KU-618-773

ICELAND
POCKET GUIDE

Walking Eye
mobile app

Discover the world's best destinations with the Insight Guides Walking Eye app, available to download for free in the App Store and Google Play.

The container app provides easy access to fantastic free content on events and activities taking place in your current location or chosen destination, with the possibility of booking, as well as the regularly-updated Insight Guides travel blog: Inspire Me. In addition, you can purchase curated, premium destination guides through the app, which feature local highlights, hotel, bar, restaurant and shopping listings, an A to Z of practical information and more. Or purchase and download Insight Guides eBooks straight to your device.

TOP 10 ATTRACTIONS

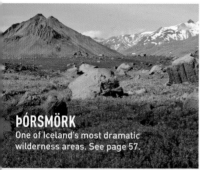

ÞÓRSMÖRK
One of Iceland's most dramatic wilderness areas. See page 57.

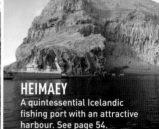

HEIMAEY
A quintessential Icelandic fishing port with an attractive harbour. See page 54.

REYKJAVÍK.
Iceland's vibrant capital has many cultural attractions. See page 25.

GEYSIR
No visit is complete without seeing Iceland's hot springs. See page 66.

GOÐAFOSS
Witness the power of these staggering falls. See page 74.

BLUE LAGOON
Bathe in the naturally heated, therapeutic waters. See page 39.

LAKE MÝVATN
A bird-watcher's paradise surrounded by volcanic peaks. See page 74.

NORTHERN LIGHTS
The most breathtaking lightshow on earth.

JÖKULSÁRLÓN
This spectacular iceberg-studded lagoon is out of this world. See page 62.

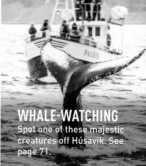

WHALE-WATCHING
Spot one of these majestic creatures off Húsavik. See page 71.

A PERFECT DAY

9.30am

Breakfast
Start the day with breakfast at your hotel or head to the retro-style café, Grái Kötturinn, on Hverfisgata 16, for orange juice, pancakes with bacon and syrup and plenty of coffee refills.

1.30pm

Reykjavík's heart
Take a walk through Austurvöllur square, the city's traditional heart, where you'll find the statue of Jón Sigurðsson, Parliament House and, adjacent, Reykjavík's modest cathedral, the Dómkirkjan. Slip past the City Hall to see the abundant birdlife on Tjörnin pond.

11.00am

Shoreline stroll
Take a morning walk past the glittering Harpa concert hall to the harbour area. If you are tempted, you could take in a whale-watching trip from one of the boats moored here. Check out Icelandic pop art at the Hafnarhús gallery and admire Mt Esja across the bay.

12.30pm

Lobster stop
Stop for a bowl of lobster soup and a beer at Sægreifinn fish shack on Geirsgata 8.

2.00pm

Heritage walk

Walk down Reykjavík's oldest street, Aðalstræti, and look in at the city's most modern heritage museum, Reykjavík 871±2 Settlement Exhibition, for some Icelandic history.

10.00pm

On the town

Austurstræti is a good place to start: the Micro Bar (no. 6) serves beer from Icelandic breweries; or grab a well-made cocktail at dressy Loftið (no. 9). Laugavegur and the surrounding streets are packed with iconic bars and clubs, such as Boston (Laugavegur 28b) and Kaffibarinn (Bergstaðastræti 1). Grab a hotdog *(pylsur)* with mustard from an all-night food stand on the way back to your hotel.

3.00pm

Retail therapy

Head to Reykjavík's main shopping street, Laugavegur, for vintage clothes (Spúútnik at 28b) and vinyl (Bad Taste at 28), along with exclusive, cutting edge fashion labels. Branching off diagonally, Skólavörðustígur is lined with beautiful art and design shops.

5.00pm

Steam and soak

Time to recover from shopping and sightseeing at one of Reykjavík's many geothermal pools. The most central is Sundhöllin, on Barónsstígur. The pool is indoor, with outdoor hot pots to relax and gossip in – the perfect way to get ready for the night ahead.

8.00pm

Fine dining

There are many excellent restaurants in the city centre. Two options for fine cosy dining are the **Ostabúðin** *(Skólavörðustíg 8)* and Skólabrú (Pósthússtræti 17), in a beautifully restored house just off Austurvöllur square.

CONTENTS

■ **Introduction**.. 10

■ **A Brief History**.. 15

■ **Where To Go**.. 25
❶ *Numbered map references pinpoint the sights*

Reykjavík.. 25
Hallgrímskirkja and Vicinity 26, Central Shopping Area 28, The Government District 29, The Harbour Area 32, Western Reykjavík 34, Eastern Reykjavík 35, Viðey and Lundey 37, The Outskirts 38

The Blue Lagoon... 39

The Golden Circle.. 40
Þingvellir 41, Skálholt 43, Geysir 44, Gullfoss 44

The West Coast... 45
Akranes 46, Borgarnes 46, Reykholt and Vicinity 46, The Snæfellsnes Peninsula 48

The West Fjords.. 50
Ísafjörður and Around 50

The Westman Islands....................................... 53
Heimaey 54

The South Coast.. 56
Þórsmörk 57, Skógar 57, Vík 59, Vatnajökull 60, Jökulsárlón 62, Höfn 62

The North Coast.. 62
Akureyri 63, Eyjafjörður 67, West of Akureyri 69, Húsavík 71

Lakes, volcanoes, canyons and falls 73
Lake Mývatn 74, Námafjall and Krafla 78, Jökulsárgljúfur 79

Eastern Iceland 80
Egilsstaðir 81, Lögurinn and Snæfell 82, The Eastfjords 82

The Interior 84
Askja and Herðubreið 85, The Sprengisandur Route 86, The Kjölur Route 88

■ **What to Do** 91

■ **Eating Out** 104

■ **A–Z Travel Tips** 115

■ **Recommended Hotels** 135

■ **Index** 142

Features

The Icelandic Horse 10
What's in a Name 12
The Sagas 18
Historical Landmarks 23
Reykjavík City Card 31
Smoky Bay's Steamy Power 37
The Parliament at Þingvellir 42
The Puffin Population 56
Whales and Whaling 72
The Ducks and Birds of Mývatn 76
Iceland's Birdlife 95
Tax-Free Shopping 100
Calendar of Events 103
Meal Times 104

INTRODUCTION

Few places on earth can match the raw and intense beauty of Iceland. Both fiery and cold, forbidding and inviting, it is a place of dramatic contrasts, home to immense ice fields, bubbling mud pools, colossal waterfalls and hot springs. Although Iceland has a long, rich cultural history, it is the land itself, sculpted by the forces of nature into a unique, ever-changing landscape, that tells the country's true story.

UNDERGROUND DRAMA

In geological terms, Iceland is a mere baby, composed of some of the youngest rocks on earth and still being formed. Over the centuries, eruptions have spewed vast fields of lava across the island's surface and projected choking clouds of ash high into the air, blocking out the sunlight and blighting crops. In 2010, the ash cloud from a volcanic eruption under Eyjafjallajökull glacier paralysed Europe's air traffic for six days; and a flare-up under Grímsvötn the following year caused more travel chaos. Every day there are thousands of minor earthquakes and shocks, most of which are only detectable by seismologists.

THE ICELANDIC HORSE

Horses have been used for transport and farming in Iceland for over 1,000 years. The country's isolation and a ban on importing new horses to keep out disease mean that its horse population is remarkably pure. Icelandic horses are relatively small but extremely tough and they can handle the rugged terrain with ease. They are found in a wide variety of colours and are respected worldwide for their intelligence, stamina and speed. The Icelandic horse has a unique gait, known as a *tölt* – a kind of running walk with a gentle flowing movement that makes for a very smooth and comfortable ride.

The presence of so much natural energy just below ground makes it possible not just to see the awesome power of nature, but to feel, hear and smell it. The limitless reserves of geothermal energy that have produced such a varied terrain also supply heat and power to Iceland's homes, and the 'rotten egg' smell of sulphur

The Seljalandsfoss Waterfall

is unmistakable whenever you turn on a hot tap. Dams across fast-flowing glacial rivers provide the nation with more than enough hydroelectrically generated power to meet its needs.

The abundant hot water not only heats homes and offices: in winter it is piped under pavements in the centre of Reykjavík to melt away the snow and ice. All year round it contributes to the social life of the Icelanders, filling outdoor swimming pools, where people meet to take a little exercise or just to chat in the hot tubs and steam rooms.

POLLUTION-FREE LAND

For Icelanders, keeping their landscape clean and pollution-free is a top priority. It is with justifiable pride that they boast that the water from any stream or non-glacial river is drinkable, due to the lack of heavy industry. Even in the capital, Reykjavík, the air is bitingly clean and light pollution is minimal – when the northern lights are in full flow, they can be seen from the city. You won't see rubbish tipped at the wayside here, nor will you encounter widespread burning of fossil fuels. There are several foreign aluminium smelters in the country, drawn by Iceland's cheap energy; however, the last dam and smelter to be built roused huge controversy, and plans to build are not certain.

HIGH STANDARD OF LIVING

Iceland is a European nation, although it remains outside the European Union mainly to protect its economically vital fishing grounds. It has strong social institutions and a well-funded welfare system. Few Icelanders are conspicuously rich, but there's little urban poverty, and the standard of living throughout the country is high.

Geographically equal in size to England, Iceland has just 332,000 inhabitants, two-thirds of whom live in the capital and its sprawling suburbs. Icelanders have a powerful respect for nature and know they can never expect to control it or have it all to themselves. The shy Arctic fox and the reindeer are rarely seen, but sheep are plentiful, and horses are widely kept. Millions of seabirds flock to the country's cliff tops and coastal meadows to nest during the bright summer months, while offshore, whales, dolphins and seals are abundant in some of the cleanest waters on earth.

WHAT'S IN A NAME

According to tradition, Iceland owes its name to a Viking adventurer who chanced upon it around AD870. After spending a long hard winter watching his cattle die from the bitter cold and lack of good grazing, he climbed a mountain only to see the fjord choked with drift ice. Wholly disenchanted, he named the place Ísland, literally 'ice land', and promptly departed for the positively balmy climes of his native Norway. Four years later one of his compatriots returned and started the first proper settlement at a place he called Reykjavík, or 'smoky bay', after the plumes of steam he saw rising from nearby thermal springs.

Icelanders make the most of the many benefits of their extraordinary environment, spending as much time as possible outdoors during the long summer days. Walking, climbing and horseriding are popular pursuits, and, as the importance of tourism has grown, so too has the number of companies offering snowmobiling on the glaciers, hiking adventures in the interior and whale-watching off the coast.

Making friends on a farm

REYKJAVÍK

Dominated by brightly painted buildings and a massive central church, Reykjavík is a lively place. Here a modern, cosmopolitan city has evolved beneath the snow-capped mountains. The population may be small, but it is clear from the cafés, restaurants and nightclubs that this is a place where people know how to have a good time. However, the scene starts late, and the often eye-watering prices for alcohol and a decent meal force many locals to get their eating and a fair bit of their drinking done at home before they venture out.

Outside the capital, some towns, notably Akureyri in the north, share some of Reykjavík's energy, but most are happy not even to try. The smaller towns are quiet, compact and neat, often no more than a cluster of colourful houses around a church or shop. The pace of life is slow, and the sense of community strong.

Plates apart

Iceland straddles the North Atlantic Ridge where two of the tectonic plates making up the Earth's surface are slowly drifting apart. The country is widening at a rate of roughly 2cm (0.8in) annually. Along this fault line, from the northeast to the southwest, earthquakes and volcanic activity are commonplace.

HOT SPRINGS AND OUTDOOR BATHS

Since the late 1970s the country's only major road, a vast circular route around the coast, has linked village to town and countryside to capital. Most communities are found on or near the ring road, a short distance from the sea, where the land is at its flattest and most fertile. This narrow coastal plain, the only truly habitable part of the country, makes up just one-fifth of Iceland's total area.

Fortunately, much of the most impressive scenery is easily accessible from the ring road. The site of the original Geysir, which gave its name to all geysers around the world, is close to the capital, as is the best outdoor bath on the planet, the Blue Lagoon. The mighty Vatnajökull glacier, the largest in Europe at 8,400 sq km (3,200 sq miles), reaches down to the sea across the southeast of the country.

To the north, Jökulsárgljúfur (now part of the Vatnajökull National Park) is not only an impressive tongue-twister, even by Icelandic standards, but also home to Europe's largest, most powerful waterfall, Dettifoss, which plummets into the canyon below amid clouds of rainbow-coloured spray. In the north and west, the coastline is splintered by craggy fjords and the sheer granite sides of flat tabletop mountains. Further inland, wide valleys rise towards the barren upland plateaux that constitute the interior. This is Europe's last wilderness, a wide expanse of bleak grey lava desert fringed by volcanoes, glaciers and mountaintops.

A BRIEF HISTORY

While elsewhere in Europe, civilisations, empires and dynasties came and went, Iceland remained uninhabited and undiscovered. It wasn't until the 8th century AD that Irish monks became the first people known to have set foot on the island, relishing its solitude. They left no physical trace behind either (though some crosses in south Iceland appear to be stylistically related to crosses from western Scotland), nor, being all men, any new generation. Within 100 years the peace they had enjoyed was no longer: the Vikings were coming. Much of Iceland's history was chronicled within a few hundred years of the events happening. The *Landnámabók* (Book of Settlements), probably written in the 12th century, describes in detail the first permanent inhabitants. The sagas, dramatic fictional tales of early Iceland penned 100 years later, add a lot more colour to the story.

Viking relics

THE FIRST SETTLERS

The country's first settlers were Norwegians, thought to have been escaping political persecution and economic hardship at home. They found Iceland by accident, having already colonised parts of both Scotland and the Faroe Islands. The official 'First Settler' was Ingólfur Arnarson, who enjoyed his first winter so much that in

874 he went to fetch his extended family and friends to come and join him. His foster brother Hjörleifur fared less well in the new land: his Irish slaves mutinied and murdered him, fleeing to the Westman Islands after committing their crime. However, there was no indigenous population for the colonisers to evict or butcher, and the biggest threat they faced was from the elements.

These first Icelanders established farms in the rather more hospitable parts of the country, and within 60 years there were approximately 25,000 people living around the coast. Some basic laws were already in place: a man could claim as much land as he could light bonfires around in one day, so long as each new fire could be seen from the previous one. Women could have as much land as a heifer could walk around in a day. Inevitably disputes broke out, which the local chieftains had to resolve. When they failed, there could be bloody battles.

THE FIRST PARLIAMENT

In AD 930 the chieftains got together and agreed on a relatively democratic system of government. A Commonwealth was established, with a national assembly or *Alþingi* meeting for two weeks every summer at Þingvellir. Here, new laws would be agreed and infringements of old laws settled by a system of regional courts. The worst punishment was to be declared an outlaw and banished from the country.

The system wasn't perfect, and there were still some bloody battles – these were, after all, the descendants of

Name-drop

Although many Icelanders can trace their families back to the early settlers, family names do not exist. Instead, children absorb their father's first name into their own. A man named Eiríkur Gúðbrandsson might, for example, have a son named Leifur Eiríksson and a daughter named Þórdís Eiríksdóttir.

Vikings, who valued courage and honour above all else. Nonetheless this period is now considered to have been a Golden Age, the Saga Age, full of great heroes and wise men.

FROM PAGANS TO CHRISTIANS

Soon, however, things were to change dramatically. Christianity had spread to northern Europe, and the zealous, if bloodthirsty, King Ólafur Tryggvason of Norway wanted Iceland for the new religion too. When his missionaries encountered resistance in the late 10th century he was all

Illustration from Njáls Saga

for butchering the entire population until the Icelandic chieftain Gizur the White promised to have another go by more peaceful means. Fortunately the lawspeaker, who presided over the Alþingi, was at that time the widely respected Þorgeir. He persuaded both sides to agree to accept his decision in advance and then went off to meditate. He came back and announced that Iceland would become Christian, although pagans could continue to practise their beliefs in private.

Bishoprics, monasteries and schools quickly followed, and books were soon being written for the first time. As a sign of their independence, the writers chose to do their work in Icelandic, not Latin. There were so few foreign influences in the centuries to come that the language they used is almost identical to the Icelandic spoken today.

All was not well in the land, however, and Iceland was about to enter its Dark Age. The Hekla volcano outside Reykjavík erupted in 1104, burying nearby farms; over-grazing and soil erosion from excessive tree-felling further reduced the amount of viable land. At the same time the church became greedy and, by imposing tithes, it split the formerly egalitarian society. Some chiefs, who were given church lands or made into senior clergy, found themselves increasingly rich and powerful. Before long the most important families started fighting for supremacy. The Alþingi, which had relied on people voluntarily accepting its authority, was now powerless to respond.

THE SAGAS

Between the 12th and 15th centuries some of the great stories the Icelanders had previously passed on from generation to generation were written down. Collectively known as The Sagas (literally 'things told'), they are universally acknowledged as one of the world's most important bodies of medieval literature. Scholars argue about how accurate they are, but for complex characters and subtle storytelling they are unbeatable. Families are torn apart by feuds, cursed heroes are doomed to exile, formidable men and women meet their ends defiant. The sagas are written in an unemotional style that makes the brutal fates of many of their characters even more shocking. The manuscripts were collected for posterity by Árni Magnússon (1663–1730) and taken off to Copenhagen for safety, but most were then lost in a terrible fire. Árni himself braved the flames to rescue some of them. The surviving Sagas weren't returned to Iceland until long after Independence. Perhaps wary of their troubled history, the authorities in Reykjavík keep the majority under lock and key, although some are on display at the Culture House.

CIVIL WAR AND BLACK DEATH

Soon the country was in a state of civil war, which only ended when Norway took sovereignty to help maintain order in 1262. Iceland kept many of its old laws, but 700 years of foreign domination had begun.

Jón Sigurðsson, leader of the independence movement

Revolts and skirmishes continued, while nature also took its toll. Long, harsh winters destroyed farm animals and crops, yet more eruptions covered parts of the country in ash, and the Black Death arrived in Iceland, laying waste to almost a third of the population.

Those Icelanders still living were too busy struggling to survive to notice that Denmark had taken over the Norwegian throne and was therefore their new master. But the Danes took little interest in their new acquisition, despite it possessing something the rest of Europe suddenly wanted: cod. Fishing brought new wealth to coastal landowners, but it brought new trouble, too.

English and German adventurers started appearing offshore, fighting among themselves, indulging in piracy and trying to control the trade in dried cod. The English got the upper hand, and this became known as the English Century.

The Danes eventually realised that they were losing out financially. When Denmark tried to ban the English from the country, the latter killed the governor and started bringing in their canons. By 1532, however, the tide had turned, and the English leader was killed in renewed fighting with Germany. However, from then on England let the Danes and

> ### National hero
>
> Jón Sigurðsson (1811–69) is a great hero to Icelanders. A scholar and MP, he agitated for independence from Denmark. He helped to achieve limited home rule, but died in 1879, long before sovereignty was restored in 1918.

the Germans fight among themselves and turned their attentions elsewhere.

THE REFORMATION

The Church was still a dominant force in the early 16th century, and when Scandinavia turned Lutheran during the 1530s it was inevitable that Iceland would soon follow suit. By the middle of the 16th century the transition had taken place, and Protestant Reformation had been well and truly imposed on an unwilling Icelandic population.

By this time, Denmark was gaining increased political authority over Iceland, and eventually complete control of the country was passed to Copenhagen. From 1602 all of Iceland's trade had to pass by law through a small group of Danish firms, a move that effectively bankrupted the country. Smallpox then wiped out almost a third of the impoverished population, and, just when it seemed as if matters could not get any worse, thousands more citizens were killed in 1783–4 by massive eruptions that poisoned almost the entire country and caused widespread famine. Denmark considered evacuating the whole surviving population, but decided instead to relax the trading laws a little and give the country a chance to recover.

As it did so, educated Icelanders looked to continental Europe and saw democracy stirring in once-powerful monarchies. Jónas Hallgrímsson, a poet, and Jón Sigurðsson (see box), a historian, started a fledgling independence movement. By 1843 they succeeded in getting the Alþingi revived as a consultative assembly – it had been suspended since 1800. A decade later trade was freed up completely. Slowly, prosperity started to return.

In 1874, Denmark, now a constitutional monarchy, returned full legislative powers to the Alþingi. The tithe system was abolished, schooling became compulsory, and the fishing industry was allowed to grow and prosper. By 1900, Iceland had its own political parties. In 1904 it was granted Home Rule and in 1918 gained independence, though it kept the Danish king as monarch.

WAR AND PEACE

Iceland, now trading with England and Germany, was neutral in World War I, although the Great Depression of the 1930s hit its growing economy. In World War II, control of the North Atlantic was a key strategic objective, and first Britain, then the United States, landed forces in Iceland. Denmark was invaded by Germany in 1940: left to its own devices, Iceland declared itself a republic in 1944.

A young Icelander

Iceland's strategic location made the new government feel nervous as the Cold War gripped the western world. In response, it joined the UN and then NATO. Still, the decision to allow US forces to return to their wartime bases in 1951 provoked riots in Reykjavík.

When Iceland next went to war, however, it was with a fellow NATO country, Britain.

The so-called Cod Wars, that came and went for 30 years after 1952, were no more than a bit of naval muscle flexing. Britain objected to successive extensions to Iceland's territorial waters and sent patrol boats to protect its trawlers. In 1975 it ordered its frigates to ram Icelandic coastguard ships, which had been cutting the cables of British trawlers. Eventually, in 1982, Iceland got its way, and 325km (200-mile) limits became the norm worldwide.

Since the last quarter of the 20th century the country has been increasingly outward looking, attracting foreign businesses and visitors. In 1986 the world's media descended on Reykjavík for a nuclear summit between presidents Reagan and Gorbachev.

Although the European Union's stringent fisheries policy has deterred Iceland from joining that group, all argument was rendered void after the 2008 worldwide economic crisis, prompting Iceland to apply for EU membership in the hopes of greater financial security. However, it was never a popular move, and the 2013 election to power of a centre-right coalition government was widely interpreted as a big 'no' to EU membership. Two years later, the new government formally withdrew Iceland's application for EU membership.

Although Iceland's economy remains dependent on fishing, the government is keen to diversify, as shown by the controversial hydroelectrically powered aluminium smelting plant in the Eastfjords and the hunt for oil around Jan Mayen Island. Tourism has also seen something of a boom in recent years, with tourist numbers increasing annually by 30 percent between 2010 and 2015. Overall, Iceland looks to the future as a proud and independent nation, happy to cooperate with the world community – but reluctant to be dictated to by it.

HISTORICAL LANDMARKS

c.8th century AD Irish monks start to settle on 'Thule'.

c.870 A Norwegian, Hrafna-Flóki, tries to settle in the West Fjords, calling the land *Ísland* (Iceland).

874 Ingólfur Arnarson and his family and friends settle on Iceland.

1000 Christianity is adopted as Iceland's official religion.

13th–14th centuries Norway and Denmark feud over ruling of Iceland.

1389 Huge eruption of Mt Hekla, followed by the Black Death.

15th century England and Germany battle to control the cod trade.

1662–1854 Trade monopoly with Denmark.

1783 Eruption of Lakagígar craters poisons land and leads to famine.

1800 Danish King abolishes the Alþingi; it is reinstated in 1843.

1874 Denmark gives the Alþingi autonomy over domestic affairs.

1918 Iceland made a sovereign state, under the Danish monarch.

1944 Independence from Denmark declared on 17 June.

1952–75 Cod Wars (1952, 1958, 1972, 1975) with the UK.

1955 Halldór Laxness wins the Nobel Prize for Literature.

1963 Surtsey Island created by an underwater volcanic eruption.

1973 Volcanic eruption on Heimaey Island.

1986 Nuclear summit between presidents Reagan and Gorbachev held in Reykjavík.

1994 Iceland enters the European Economic Area.

2000 Mt Hekla eruption in February; earthquakes in June.

2006 Iceland resumes commercial whaling.

2010 Eyjafjallajökull erupts, bringing Europe's air traffic to a standstill.

2013 Iceland grants two oil-exploration licences for its portion of the Jan Mayen Ridge.

2015 Iceland's application for EU membership is withdrawn; the Bárðarbunga volcano erupts.

2016 Historian Guðni Thorlacius Jóhannesson (b.1968) becomes Iceland's youngest president. The Icelandic national football team capture the imagination of the world by reaching the quarterfinals of Euro 2016, knocking out England in the process.

WHERE TO GO

Iceland is one of the world's most spectacular destinations, with vast empty landscapes illuminated by sparkling, clear, sub-arctic air and cosy fishing villages sheltering from Atlantic storms beneath gargantuan cliffs. It is a paradise for anyone with a love of nature and the great outdoors, lent a surreal edge by its lunar landscape and the ever-restless tectonic activity below.

Visitors range from the experienced adventure traveller in search of new challenges to those on a two- or three-day stopover between Europe and North America. Whether you come for several weeks or just a few days, there will be no shortage of things to see and do. Iceland's infrastructure is well designed and efficient, making independent travel almost as easy as taking one of the many commercial tours and excursions.

Iceland works almost exclusively in English, so a lack of Icelandic is not usually a problem. Facilities are constantly improving, and the number of people visiting Iceland means there is usually a range of options when it comes to choosing tours or means of transport.

REYKJAVÍK

Most visitors start and end their trip in **Reykjavík** ❶, and many are surprised by how small and insubstantial it can seem. There are virtually no high-rise buildings, certainly there are no skyscrapers, and the use of corrugated iron and timber in many of the buildings makes them

North and west

Reykjavík is the world's most northerly capital city, at 64.08°N, and at 21.55°W it is Europe's most westerly capital.

Kirkjufellsfoss, also known as Church Mountain Falls, located on the north side of the Snaefellsnes Peninsula

Stopping to admire the view at Tjörnin lake

look almost temporary. In fact, the building materials and layout of the city are very practical and, like everything else in Iceland, are designed with the elements in mind.

Reykjavík is a destination in its own right. Over a third of the country's population live in the capital, where they enjoy fresh air and a magnificent location between the bay and the mountains and glaciers of the interior. Apart from a few major roads around the edge of town, the streets are narrow and sometimes steep. The city's energetic and distinctive cultural scene is a constant source of fascination, yet it retains a certain slow pace and almost rustic charm that makes it unique among the world's capitals. Moreover, everything you will want to see is either within walking distance or a short bus or taxi ride away.

HALLGRÍMSKIRKJA AND VICINITY

The central importance of the massive **Hallgrímskirkja Ⓐ** (off Bergþórugata; www.hallgrimskirkja.is, daily June–Sept 9am–9pm, Oct–May 9am–5pm; free except for tower) is quickly revealed on the drive into the capital across the lava fields from the airport to the south. The church is so enormous that it not only dominates the skyline, it reduces everything else to virtual insignificance. The eye is constantly drawn back to it and its bizarre shape resembling a rocket ready for lift-off. The church is the most obvious place to begin a visit to Reykjavík, and you will almost certainly approach it up Skólavörðustígur. As you head uphill on this street, take time to look in the windows of the enticing galleries and bijoux boutiques, reflecting how much artistic talent such a small country has produced.

A lift runs up the Hallgrímskirkja's 73 metre (240ft) tower – with a few stairs at the end – from where you are rewarded with the best view of Reykjavík from the viewing platform. Designed by Guðjón Samúelsson, it is a monument not only to Christ, but also to Reykjavík's belief that being a small city need not limit its ambitions. The church itself is very bare, as befits its Lutheran status, and there is not much to see except the magnificent **organ**, which is 15 metres (50ft) high and has more than 5,000 pipes.

Just outside the church is a **statue of Leifur Eiríksson**, Iceland's greatest adventurer, who reached America long before Christopher Colum-

bus. The statue, which is by *Statue of Leifur Eiríksson*

Alexander Stirling Calder, was a gift from the US government to mark the Icelandic parliament's 1,000th anniversary in 1930.

Nearby is a museum dedicated to Einar Jónsson (1874–1954), one of Iceland's greatest modern exponents of sculpture and the master

Reykjavík rooftops

of symbolism and epic: the **Safn Einars Jónssonar** Ⓑ (Einar Jónsson Museum; Njarðargata; www.lej.is; Tue–Sun 10am–5pm). Jónsson was virtually a recluse towards the end of his life and many of the 100 or so pieces exhibited here are dark and sombre in character. At the back of the building, on Freyjugata, the small sculpture garden is open year-round.

CENTRAL SHOPPING AREA

Returning to the bottom of Skólavörðustígur brings you to Reykjavík's main shopping street, **Laugavegur**. The name translates literally as 'Hot Spring Road', and it means what it says – it was once the path taken by townspeople who were going to do their washing in the hot pools in Laugardalur (see page 36). Today, thanks to the city's unique geothermal heating system, the same source is used to help to keep pavements and car parks ice-free in winter, using underground water piped up from the Laugarnes boreholes. The street is home to a mixture of international shops, local stores, cafés, bars, restaurants and hotels... plus the world's only penis collection at the **Icelandic Phallological Museum** **ⓒ** (Laugavegur 116; http://phallus.is; daily 10am–6pm). On display are over 200 specimens from almost every mammal found in Iceland or in its waters; four human donors have bequeathed their members to the museum.

Higher-minded souls will find greater pleasure at **Þjóðmenningarhúsið** **ⓓ** (Culture House, Hverfisgata 15; www.culturehouse.is; May–15 Sept daily 11am–5pm; winter closed Mon). The key exhibit is a fascinating collection of medieval manuscripts containing rare sagas and *eddas* full of details of life in Iceland and elsewhere in northern Europe from the time of the Vikings onwards. There is also a collection of memorabilia from the struggle for independence. It is all housed in a splendid building, opened in 1909, that was initially intended for the National Library.

THE GOVERNMENT DISTRICT

At the western end of the main shopping street, after its name changes to Bankastræti, is the government district – **Government House** is not open to the public but is nonetheless well worth a look from the outside. It is one of the oldest houses in the country, dating from 1761 when it was built as a prison. It now houses the offices of the Prime Minister.

Across Hverfisgata, standing on a hillock, is an imposing **statue of Ingólfur Arnarson**,

Shopping in Laugavegur

Walking in Austurvöllur

the first settler, looking out over the Atlantic. Behind him is the National Theatre and to his right are some of the government ministries.

The Icelandic parliament has only 63 members, so its headquarters, **Alþingishúsið** Ⓔ (not open to the public), is a well-proportioned but unassuming grey basalt mansion (1881) on Austurvöllur. In between 2008–16, archaeological digs around the building have unearthed the first Viking-Age industrial site found in Iceland: an iron smithy and fish- and wool-processing facilities were once located here. When parliament is sitting, its debates can be observed from the public gallery; but they are, of course, in Icelandic.

Alongside Alþingishúsið is Reykjavík's stone and corrugated iron Lutheran cathedral, **Dómkirkjan** Ⓕ (http://domkirkjan.is; Mon–Fri 10am–4.30pm; during ceremonies at weekend), built in 1785, which has a rather plain facade, and a trim, galleried interior with arched windows that bathe the place in light.

The grassy square in front of the parliament, **Austurvöllur**, is popular with picnickers in summer. One of the great campaigners for independence keeps a watchful eye over proceedings: the **statue of Jón Sigurðsson,** known as *The Pride of Iceland,* rises above the square. A couple of streets away is another square, **Lækjartorg,** where you'll find one of the two city bus stations.

The most tangible signs of Iceland's Viking settlement can be seen at the **Reykjavík 871±2 Settlement**

Exhibition ⑤ (Landnámssýningin; www.reykjavik 871.is; daily 9am–8pm; guided tours June–Aug Sat–Sun at 11am) at Aðalstræti 16. Here you will find the remains of an oval-shaped Viking-Age farmhouse just below the current street level, along with one of the country's most impressive and imaginative exhibitions. The city's main tourist office is at the end of the road.

Just to the west, on the banks of **Tjörnin** ⑥, a city-centre lake, is **Raðhús** ⑦ (Reykjavík City Hall, corner of Tjarnargata and Vonarstræti; Mon–Fri 8am–7pm, Sat–Sun noon–6pm; free). This modern glass-and-concrete construction, designed to link the people with their politicians and the city buildings with the lake, is a key example of 20th-century Icelandic architecture. It has a café, an exhibition space and a large relief map of Iceland.

Alongside the lake is **Listasafn Íslands** ⑧ (National Gallery of Iceland, Fríkirkjuvegur 7; www.listasafn.is; daily mid-May–mid-Sept 10am–5pm, rest of the year Tue–Sun 11am–5pm). This small gallery has a fine permanent collection of work by Icelandic artists, including the country's first

REYKJAVÍK CITY CARD

Consider investing in a Reykjavík Welcome Card; which can be purchased from tourist offices, bus terminals, museums, the City Hall Information Desk and many hotels for a cost of ISK3,500 for 24 hours, ISK4,700 for 48 hours and ISK5,500 for 72 hours. The card gives access to a great selection of museums and galleries, the Family Park and Zoo and all of the city's swimming pools. It also allows unlimited free travel on the city buses and a ferry trip to Viðey Island, plus discounts in some shops and restaurants and on some tours.

professional painter Ásgrímur Jónsson (1876–1958). There is a café on the first floor with internet access. A couple of blocks away is a very different kind of visual experience, the **Volcano House** Ⓚ (Tryggvagata 11; www.volcanohouse.is; tel: 555 1900; daily 10am–10pm, shows on the hour). The films show 50 years of Icelandic volcanic eruptions, captured on film by the cinema's owner. Films are in English, French and German at different times of the day and show dramatic pictures of eruptions, including the one in 1964 that created Iceland's newest island, Surtsey.

THE HARBOUR AREA

Just north of the government district are the few streets that lead up to the harbour. These are full of cafés, bars and restaurants and are great for just wandering around. Hafnarstræti was once the old quayside and contains some

Jón Gunnar Árnason's stainless steel Sólfar (Sun Voyager)

of the city's oldest buildings; many of these have been beautifully restored. The Uno restaurant, Hafnarstræti 1–3, for example, was once the **Fálkahúsið**, where the king of Denmark kept his prize falcons. There are two carved wooden falcons on the roof to commemorate the fact. On Tryggvagata is **Hafnarhús**  (Harbour

Whaling ships, Reykjavík harbour

House Art Museum; www.artmuseum.is; daily 10am–5pm; Thu until 10pm), one of three galleries belonging to the Reykjavík Art Museum, situated in the stylishly renovated former warehouse of the Port of Reykjavík. Here you will find on display a large collection by the internationally renowned Icelandic pop artist, Erró, as well as other contemporary artists from Iceland and elsewhere.

The modern **harbour** itself, built on reclaimed land, is still operational, with fishing boats bringing in their catch. In a good example of Icelandic contrariness, the **whale-watching boats** belonging to Elding (tel: 519 5000; www.elding.is) and **Special Tours** (tel: 560 8800, www.specialtours.is) share the dockside with **whaling ships**, recognisable from their black hulls and a red H on their funnels.

Next to the harbour is **Harpa Concert Hall**  (tel: 528 5000; http://en.harpa.is; building open daily 10am–midnight, box office open Mon–Fri 10am–6pm, Sat–Sun noon–6pm), opened in 2011 and two years later won the European Union Prize for Contemporary Architecture – the Mies van der Rohe Award. Its glittering exterior, designed by artist Ólafur Elíasson to resemble the mosaic-like basalt columns found scattered throughout Iceland, reflects the sea and sky in a kaleidoscopic lightshow.

Along the bay to the east is Jón Gunnar Árnason's stunning sculpture *Sólfar* (*Sun Voyager*; 1986), which is based on a classic Viking longboat.

WESTERN REYKJAVÍK

You will probably arrive in western Reykjavík where the bus terminals and domestic airport are situated, but there is little to tempt you out there again before your departure. The main exception is the excellent **Þjóðminjasafn Íslands ⓝ** (National Museum, Hringbraut, Suðurgata 1, junction with Hringbraut; www.thjodminjasafn.is; May–mid-Sept daily 10am–5pm, mid-Sept–Apr Tue–Sun 10am–5pm), which provides comprehensive insight into the past 1,200 years of Icelandic history. The section on the use of DNA testing is particularly interesting, detailing research work done on the teeth of the first settlers in order to determine their origins.

While in the vicinity, have a look too at **Norræna Húsið ⓞ** (Nordic House, Sturlugata 5; www.nordichouse.is; daily 11am–5pm; free except for some exhibitions), a Scandinavian cultural centre with a well-stocked library offering free internet access, exhibitions, concerts and a café.

On the other side of the domestic airport, on **Öskjuhlíð** hill, is the glass-domed **Perlan ⓟ** (Pearl), a revolving restaurant that sits atop six enormous tanks used to store the geothermally heated water that supplies the city. The tanks hold 24 million litres (over 5 million gallons) of hot water and cater for almost half of Reykjavík's water consumption. Öskjuhlíð itself is a leafy area thanks to tree-planting schemes and the creation of walking and cycling paths.

Inside the Perlan building, the **Sögusafnið** (Saga Museum; www.sagamuseum.is; daily 10am–6pm) is a great place to

Nauthólsvík beach

take older children. This is Iceland's equivalent of Madame Tussaud's and an absorbing collection of life-size silicon models of the main characters from the sagas, which really brings the country's medieval history to life.

At the southern edge of Öskjuhlíð is a seawater lagoon with its own mini-beach, **Nauthólsvík ⓠ** (www.nautholsvik. is; mid-May–mid-Aug daily 10am–7pm, mid Aug–mid-May Tue, Thu and Fri 11am–1pm, Mon and Wed also 5–7.30pm, Sat 11am–3pm), where the water is heated by the addition of hot water from the hill. The seawater reaches 20°C (68°F), and there is a geothermal hot pot that gets even hotter (up to 35°C/95°F).

EASTERN REYKJAVÍK

There is more to see on the eastern side of the city. By the sea, isolated on a grassy square, is **Höfði House ⓡ**. The building is used for government receptions and social functions and hence closed to the public. Höfði was the location for the

Inside the Ásmundarsafn, the Ásmundur Sveinsson Sculpture Museum

summit meetings in 1986 between presidents Reagan and Gorbachev to discuss global disarmament. A ghost supposedly haunts the house, but an electrical fault rather than the troublesome spectre was blamed for the fire that damaged the building in 2009.

Inland is **Kjarvalsstaðir** ⑤ (Municipal Gallery, Flókagata; http://artmuseum.is/kjarval sstadir; daily 10am–5pm), another part of the Reykjavík Art Museum. Half the gallery is dedicated to the huge, colourful, often abstract landscapes by the Icelandic artist Jóhannes Kjarval (1885–1972), while the other half houses visiting exhibitions. Further east is **Ásmundarsafn** ⑦ (Ásmundur Sveinsson Sculpture Museum, Sigtún 105; http://artmuseum.is/asmundarsafn; daily May–Sept 10am–5pm, Oct–Apr 1–5pm, outdoor sculpture garden open 24-hours), a third part of the Reykjavík Art Museum. This is modern sculpture at its best, with huge figures depicting the people of Iceland as well as mythical characters.

A short distance to the east is the **Laugardalur** ⓤ area, a green belt that serves as the capital's main sports area, with a large, open-air, geothermally heated swimming pool, soccer stadium, sports hall and ice-skating rink. There are also the Viking-themed mini-rides of the **Family Park** and the adjoining **Reykjavík Zoo** (www.mu.is; park and zoo daily 10am–5pm, until 6pm in summer), which contains domestic farm animals, Arctic foxes, mink, reindeers, seals and a small cold water aquarium. The nearby **Botanical Gardens** (daily May–Sept 10am–10pm, Oct–Apr 10am–3pm; free) have an impressive collection of 5,000 plants and almost all of Iceland's flora.

VIÐEY AND LUNDEY

Just 1km (0.6 miles) out to sea due north of Reykjavík is the island of **Viðey Ⓥ**, a haunting and historically significant place full of tussocked grass and soughing wind. Just up from the jetty is the oldest stone building in Iceland, Viðeyjarstofa, built in 1755 and now containing a summertime cafe. The bird life is prolific on Viðey, and there are some impressive basalt columns on the isthmus at the centre of the island, as well as some modern sculptures including Yoko Ono's Imagine Peace Tower, which lights up the sky on significant dates. Viðey is small enough to stroll around in an hour or two. Ferries depart from Sundahöfn harbour (Skarfabakki pier) in Reykjavík between mid-May and August at hourly intervals (for times, tel: 533 5055), and the trip takes less than 10 minutes.

SMOKY BAY'S STEAMY POWER

The name Reykjavík, meaning 'smoky bay', was coined by one of the early settlers who mistook the steam rising from the ground for smoke. Inevitably the arrival of man brought pollution in its wake, especially with the burning of fossil fuels. As the city massively expanded in the 20th century, so did the threat from polluted air. The decision, taken in the 1960s, to convert the city to environmentally friendly power sources cut carbon dioxide emissions from the heating system alone from 270,000 tonnes a year to virtually zero. Today, the geothermally heated water that gave the city its name is used to heat its buildings and is even piped beneath the pavements in winter to prevent icing. Reykjavík is arguably the world's greenest capital city.

The Blue Lagoon

The best chance of seeing puffins close to the capital is on the tiny island of **Lundey**. Whale-watching tours (see page 33) sail past between mid-May and mid-August.

THE OUTSKIRTS

Just outside Reykjavík there are a number of sights that can be visited on a short bus or taxi journey. To the east is **Árbæjarsafn** Ⓦ (Arbær Open-Air Museum; http://borgarso gusafn.is; daily June–Aug 10am–5pm, Sept–May tours at 1pm, no booking needed). The original farm was mentioned in the sagas and is now a showcase for how Icelanders used to live. There are old homesteads with turf roofs, mostly relocated from the city centre, and a church that dates from 1842.

Another must-see is the nearby **Living Art Museum** (Völvufell 13-21; www.nylo.is; Tue–Fri noon–5pm, only during exhibitions Sat–Sun 1–5pm; free), located in a splendid new building.

To the west is the town of **Hafnarfjörður** ❷, which was once a bigger port than Reykjavík, but is now considered more-or-less a suburb of the capital. The location is attractive, with parks and cliffs by the sea. **Fjörukráin** (Viking Village, Strandgata 50; www.fjorukrain.is) houses a guesthouse and the nation's only Viking restaurant. The best time to come here is in February when Viking-clad waiters serve traditional foods such as pickled rams' testicles and cured sharkmeat.

Hafnarborg Arts Centre (Strandgata 34; www.hafnarborg. is; Wed–Mon noon–5pm) is a genuine highlight of the town and has exhibitions by Icelandic and international artists, as well as occasional music recitals.

Hafnarfjörður Museum (www.visithafnarfjordur.is) is based across four separate sites: the two main buildings are **Pakkhúsið** (Vesturgata 8; June–Aug daily 11am–5pm), which contains an interesting canter through the town's history and a little toy museum; and **Sívertens-Hús** (next door; June–Aug daily 11am–5pm), the 19th-century home of local bigwig, Bjarni Sívertsen. There is a fine church and a **sculpture garden** at Viðistaðir on the northern outskirts of the town.

THE BLUE LAGOON

One trip out of Reykjavík that should not be missed is to the world's greatest outdoor bath, **Bláa Lonið ③** (Blue Lagoon, Grindavík; tel: 420 8800; www.bluelagoon.com; daily June–21 Aug 8am–midnight, 17–31 May and 22–31 Aug 8am–10pm, 2–16 May Mon, Tue, Wed, Thu 9am–8pm, Fri, Sat, Sun 8am–9pm, Sep–Oct Mon, Tue, Wed 8am–8pm, Thu, Fri, Sat, Sun 8am–10pm, daily Nov–Apr 8am–8pm; pre-booking is required). Most hotels will have details of tours, but you can also arrive by public bus. The lagoon is a pool of seawater naturally heated by

Popular place

Reykjavík is increasingly popular as a destination for cruise ships. Over 90,000 visitors a year come to Iceland this way. The vessels moor in the main harbour.

the geothermal activity below the surface. It sits in the middle of a lava field and you can lounge around here with warm mud oozing between your toes in wonderfully warm water temperatures of 37–40°C (98–104°F) all year round.

In spite of its name, the lagoon is not a natural phenomenon, but a fortuitous by-product of Iceland's geo-thermal energy usage. The nearby Svartsengi power plant pumps mineral-laden water from up to 2km (1.2 miles) beneath the earth's surface, at a temperature of 240°C (470°F). The superheated water passes through a dual process, on the one hand to generate electricity, and on the other to heat fresh water. This run-off water, rich in silica, salt and other elements, once flowed out into a pool a few hundred metres from the present lagoon's site. Psoriasis and eczema sufferers noticed that bathing in the water seemed to ease their symptoms. Once the word was out, the lagoon was moved to its current location, and state-of-the-art facilities, carefully designed to complement the surrounding landscape, were built around it.

A cave-like sauna is carved into the lava and a thundering waterfall delivers a pounding massage. The complex also contains a spa treatment area, restaurant, snack bar, shop, conference facilities, and, should you care to spend the night, there is a guesthouse just over the lava field. All summer long (June–Aug), however, the changing rooms get crowded and it may be worth getting up early to beat the crowds. If you are impressed by the Blue Lagoon's healing properties, a range of eponymous skin and bathing products are on sale across the island.

THE GOLDEN CIRCLE

This 300km (190-mile) round trip from Reykjavík takes in some of the key historical and geological sites in Iceland. They include the original geyser that gave its name to gushing blowholes worldwide, the site of the country's first

Þingvellir, a national park and site of the original parliament

parliament, and one of its most dramatic waterfalls. You can cover the route on any one of a number of day tours from Reykjavík. They take about seven hours, but include stops at gift shops and eating places along the way. The trip can just about be done by public transport or you could hire a car. The route is well signposted, and parking is good.

ÞINGVELLIR

The nearest landmark to the capital on the Golden Circle route is the site of the original Alþingi (parliament), established in 930. It is situated in **Þingvellir** ❹ (Assembly Plains; free), a large national park that has enormous political and geographical significance. Unfortunately, there are few actual monuments or buildings to be seen, and you have to use your imagination to picture the events of the past.

There is a well-marked **information centre** (www.thingvel lir.is; daily Nov–Mar 9am–5pm, Apr–Oct until 6pm) with a cafe and a shop selling maps and books about the area. Fishing and camping permits can be obtained here. It's worth familiarising yourself with the layout of the park before you set off to explore as it's not that well signposted.

The park is situated on top of the line where the North American and Eurasian continental plates meet. In fact they are slowly drifting apart at a rate of 2cm (0.78in) a year. Above the rift, at the **Almannagjá viewing point**, there is the interpretive **centre** (daily 9am–5pm, summer until 8pm), containing

THE PARLIAMENT AT ÞINGVELLIR

Þingvellir may feel as if it's in the middle of nowhere, but 1,000 years ago it was the focal point of the country. For two weeks every summer Icelanders flooded into the valley to take part in or just watch the proceedings of the Alþingi (parliament). The position was perfect, with plenty of grazing land for horses, good tracks from the more populated parts of Iceland and a lake teeming with fish to feed the multitudes. Trading and socialising went on continuously while the leaders got on with the serious work of running the country. It was the job of the 36 chieftains from the various regions to agree on new laws, under the supervision of the 'lawspeaker'. A Law Council, made up of four regional courts and a supreme court, dealt with infringements and disputes – outlawry was the most severe sentence that could be passed. However, once the Alþingi's judgment had been made, the system relied on the wronged party enforcing the punishment. Parliament itself had no power to stop feuds or even open warfare from breaking out when grievances could not be settled. From the mid-16th century the courts gained more power, and Þingvellir became a site of public punishment and execution, reflected in many of its grisly placenames. Men were beheaded, adulterous women drowned, and unfortunate souls convicted of witchcraft were burned alive. Alþingi's last meeting was held here in 1798; after that a national court and parliament was established in Reykjavík.

interactive displays about the national park. From up here, you can clearly see the rift valley as you look towards the lake. The red-roofed church dates from 1859. It stands on the site of a much bigger church that held sway over all the local inhabitants. Below you is the Alþingi site itself. You can walk down into it; a flagpole marks where the leader of the parliament, the law speaker, made his proclamations. Just to the east of

Inside Skálholt

the Alþingi, the Öxará River flows into a lake, **Þingvallavatn**. There's a 20 metre (66ft) waterfall, and nearby you can clearly see the layers of ash left by successive eruptions.

SKÁLHOLT

Next stop on the Golden Circle is **Skálholt ⑤**, about 45km (28 miles) to the east of Þingvellir. It is hard to imagine that this was once the biggest settlement in Iceland, as there is little to see here today; but for over 700 years, from 1056 onwards, this was a seat of enormous ecclesiastical power. A massive earthquake destroyed Skálholt's cathedral in the late 18th century, when the bishop picked up his cassock and headed for the relative safety of Reykjavík. The present church was built in 1963. Inside you can see the coffin of one of the early bishops, uncovered during the building work, and a fine modern mosaic above the altar. Iceland's oldest music festival, of early and contemporary classical music, is held here in June (www.sumartonleikar.is).

GEYSIR

Another 20km (12 miles) to the northeast you can see evidence of the one power that both church and state have to respect – nature. There are bigger geysers (*geysir* in Icelandic) in the world, and more impressive ones, but this is the original. **Geysir ❻** is one of the few Icelandic words to have made it into the lexicon of world language. Sadly, the gusher that used to reach heights of 60m (200ft) hasn't performed well for decades. For years, Icelanders poured masses of soap powder into the orifice to make it perform, but in the end they gave up. It still erupts on odd occasions, but generally only to a height of around 10 metres (33ft)

Fortunately, there is the smaller, but far more reliable **Strokkur** (literally 'the churn') beside Geysir: Strokkur spurts to a height of around 20m (66ft) every few minutes, without artificial encouragement.

The whole Geysir area is geothermically active and smells strongly of sulphur (similar to the smell rotten eggs). Walking trails are marked out among the steaming vents and glistening, multicoloured mud formations. Don't be tempted to poke your fingers into any pools: an average of seven tourists are badly burned every week during the summer months.

Strokkur

GULLFOSS

An example of nature at its most forceful is to be found another 6km (4 miles) along the road to the north. **Gullfoss ❼** (Golden Falls; http://gullfoss.is) is, in fact, two separate waterfalls a short distance apart. Their combined

Gullfoss carving out a canyon

drop is 32 metres (105ft), and the pounding water then thunders away along the 2km (1.2-mile) -long canyon below. Several paths lead above and alongside the waterfall, allowing you to get within an arm's length of the awesome flow. Wear a raincoat, or the clouds of spray that create dozens of photogenic rainbows on sunny days will douse you from head to foot.

The falls were nearly destroyed by a hydroelectric dam project in the 1920s but the plans were halted. The government instead purchased the falls and made them a national monument.

THE WEST COAST

The wild Snæfellsnes peninsula is within day-trip striking-distance of Reykjavík, and as such is a growing tourist destination. Most tour companies offer a circuit of its rocky coves, extinct glacier-topped volcano **Snæfellsjökull**, and traditional fishing villages such as Ólafsvík and Stykkishólmur. On the way, several settlements hold cultural surprises.

AKRANES

Located just north of Reykjavík, **Akranes** ❽ is dominated by fish-processing, trawler production and cement making. Far more appealing is the **Safnasvæðið á Akranesi** (Akranes Museum Centre; www.museum.is; daily mid-May–mid-Sept 10am–5pm, rest of the year by previous arrangement only), east of town. It houses a folk museum with the emphasis on maritime history, including a well-preserved *ketch*, one of the first decked fishing boats in Iceland. The museum also has the country's largest collection of rocks, minerals and fossils. There are swimming pools and four hotpots adjacent on Garðar.

BORGARNES

Borgarnes ❾ on the windswept west coast, is essentially a service centre for the neighbouring dairy farms. The park, known as **Skallagrímsgarður**, commemorates one of Iceland's first settlers, Skallagrímur Kveldúlfsson, whose burial mound is still visible. His son, Egill, was the hero of *Egils Saga*, and there is a monument to him by the mound. **The Settlement Centre of Iceland** (www.landnam.is; daily 10am–9pm), in a restored warehouse by the harbour, offers up two striking exhibitions. One explores the settlement of Iceland, and the other uses striking sound and visuals to tell the tale of Egill and his bloodthirsty deeds.

REYKHOLT AND VICINITY

Both its setting and its cultural history make **Reykholt** ❿ a place worth visiting. The wide, open spaces of its valley setting are refreshing after so many mountains and were once home to Snorri Sturluson, born in 1179 and immortalised by his saga-writing. He was a distinguished scholar but was murdered here in 1241 after falling foul of the Norwegian

Stykkishólmur harbour

king. You can visit **Snorralaug**, the bathing pool where the chieftain would receive visitors and, beside it, the partly-restored remains of a tunnel that led to his farmhouse. **Snorrastofa** (www.snorrastofa.is; May–Sept daily 10am–6pm, Oct–Apr Mon–Fri 10am–5pm), located just next to the church, is a research centre dedicated to Snorri, and contains an exhibition about his life and work.

At **Húsafell**, to the east, many Icelanders have holiday cottages from which they explore the surrounding area. Nearby is the magnificent **Hraunfossar**, a multitude of tiny cascades that tumble into the Hvíta River along a 1km (0.6-mile) stretch. Further afield is a forest and two **glaciers**, Þórisjökull and Eiríksjökull, as well as several **lava caves** hidden inside the 52km-long Hallmundarhraun lava flow, including Víðgelmir at the farm Fljótstunga (tel: 783 3600; www.thecave.is). Húsafell is also the starting point for the excursions into the heart of Iceland's second largest glacier – **Langjökull**. Into the Glacier operates tours to this unique, man-made labyrinth of 500m

(1,584-ft) -long, artificially lit corridors and caves that have been dug into the glacier's cap. See https://intotheglacier.is for more details.

Further north is the reconstructed farmhouse of **Eiríksstaðir** (www.leif.is; June–Aug daily 9am–6pm), from which the Vikings launched their westward voyages of discovery. Eirík the Red, after whom the farm is named, went on to discover Greenland, while his son, Leifur, was the first European to set foot in America. There is a reconstruction of the original farm, complete with Viking guides, next to the excavated hall; the latter dates from 890–980.

THE SNÆFELLSNES PENINSULA

At 1,445 metres (4,740ft) high, **Snæfellsjökull** ⑪ is permanently snow-capped. It was made famous worldwide by Jules Verne as the entry point for his *Journey to the Centre of the Earth* and also plays a role in *Under the Glacier,* by Nobel Prize-winning Icelandic novelist Halldór Laxness. The glacier is popular for snowmobile tours. The main peak itself is a less daunting climb than it looks, but it's best to go with gear (crampons) and a guide, due to crevasses on the glacier.

Snorralaug

From late May to August, Láki Tours run whale-watching trips (tel: 546 6808; www.lakitours.com) from **Ólafsvík**, where there's a good chance of spotting minke, white-beaked dolphin and other cetaceans. In winter (November to April), killer whales follow the herring into Grundarfjörður, and Láki sail out from the village of the same name to greet them.

A breathtaking view from Snæfellsjökull

Further along the north coast, **Stykkishólmur** ⑫ is an attractive place with brightly painted wooden houses down by the harbour. At the quayside, it's possible to take a two-hour bird-watching and scallop-tasting tour. There is an unusual modern **church** overlooking the town, its interior lit by hundreds of bulbs that seem to drip from the ceiling. Classical music concerts take place here in summer. The town's former library has an equally watery feel; the American artist Roni Horn converted into an art installation Vatnasafn (www.libraryofwater.is; June–Aug daily 11am–5pm, Sept–Mar Tue–Sat11am–5pm). South of the town is the mountain of **Helgafell**, much talked about in Icelandic folklore, but not much more than a hillock. It is said that you can have three wishes granted if you climb it in silence from the west and then descend to the east without looking back.

A car/passenger ferry sails from Stykkishólmur to the West Fjords, calling in at the delightful island of **Flatey** ⑬ in summer. It is a sleepy, peaceful little place, with restored wooden houses set among bright yellow fields of buttercups. The eastern part of the island is a **nature reserve** teeming with birdlife. Watch out for the Arctic terns, which seem particularly aggressive here – even the island's sheep aren't immune from their dive-bombing attacks. There is a fine little church, which was painted by the Catalan artist Baltasar in return for free accommodation, and, next door, the oldest and smallest library in Iceland. Overnight accommodation is available in summer.

THE WEST FJORDS

Travellers in the West Fjords face some of the worst roads in the country and the often-inhospitable climate means it is a relatively little-visited part of Iceland. Yet the region offers Iceland's most dramatic, craggy fjords and some of its best hiking, while soaring cliffs host literally millions of breeding sea birds.

ÍSAFJÖRÐUR AND AROUND

The only town of any real size in the region is **Ísafjörður** . The deep harbour helped it to become an important fishing community, and now plays host to cruise ships too. For a taste of just how tough life in these parts once was, visit the **West Fjords Heritage Museum** (Sudurtangi; www.nedsti.is; mid-May–mid-Sept daily 9am–6pm). Housed

Flatey island

in a well-restored timber warehouse, exhibits trace the development of the town and its fishing industry, with all sorts of unusual nautical paraphernalia. The town has a swimming pool, cinema and a few restaurants and hotels.

About 12km (7 miles) north, **Bolungarvík** is an exposed spot, liable to landslides and avalanches. It has a couple of little museums. The **Ósvör Maritime Museum** (www.osvor.is; June–Aug daily 10am–5pm; winter by appointment) is in a restored fishing station and the **Natural History Museum** (Aðalstræti 21; www.nabo.is; June–Aug daily 10am–5pm; winter weekdays 9am–4pm and by prior appointment only) has a jumble of stuffed animals including a seal and polar bear. Further west, the coast is largely uninhabited; the scenery is wild and imposing, a mixture of wind-lashed headlands and mighty snow-capped peaks.

Sturdy Icelandic horse

Southeast of Ísafjörður, the road winds around several fjords to the village of **Reykjanes**, which is worth a stop for its heated outdoor pool and sauna. If you want to get close to a glacier, continue towards the **Kaldalón glacial lagoon**. From the head of the lagoon you can follow a walking trail for about an hour and a half to the tip of the glacier.

The area further north towards the **Hornstrandir Peninsula** ⓯ is now uninhabited, after the last family left it in 1995. The beauty of this part of the country is astonishing with its sandy bays, rugged cliffs, meadows of wild flowers and massive bird colonies. For serious hiking it's hard to beat, and you can literally walk all day without meeting anyone. If you're lucky you might spot an Arctic fox and, offshore, whales and seals.

West of Ísafjörður, the road runs through some tiny fishing villages as it heads south. There is a breath-taking descent into **Hrafnseyri**, the birthplace of the Independence leader, Jón Sigurðsson. A small museum is dedicated to his memory (www.hrafnseyri.is; June–Aug daily 11am–6pm), and there is much celebration in the village on Independence Day, 17 June. The **Dynjandi waterfall**, meaning 'the thundering one', just south of here, is a spectacular collection of cascades.

To the west, **Tálknafjörður** is a lively spot. It has a good swimming pool, bike hire, an adventure centre offering watersports and walking, and even a bar. Up the hillside are two open-air geothermal hotpots, Pollurinn, with beautiful views of the fjord.

Látrabjarg is the most westerly point in Europe. What makes the long, pothole-filled journey worthwhile is the sense of bleakness and the plunging **bird cliffs**. Thousands of puffins nest here in burrows, and you can get surprisingly

Taking to the water near Ísafjörður

close to them. There are at
least as many guillemots,
too, plus the largest colony
of razorbills in the world. In
spite of the numbers, bird-
watching is not as easy here
as elsewhere in the country,
because the cliffs form such
a long, straight line.

Dynjandi falls

There is a wonderful **beach**
at nearby **Rauðasandur**,
with pink sand and superb
surf thundering in from the
Atlantic. **Hnjótur** is home to
the **Egill Ólafsson Museum**
(www.hnjotur.is; May–Sept daily 10am–6pm), one man's odd-
ball collection of marine rescue equipment, old telephones
and a typewriter with Icelandic characters. The prize exhibit
is a rusting Aeroflot biplane that ended up in Iceland after its
pilot, fleeing Russia, was refused permission to land in the
US. Outside is a replica Viking longship, a gift from Norway to
mark 1,100 years of settlement.

THE WESTMAN ISLANDS

The **Westman Islands** ⓖ, or *Vestmannaeyjar* to give them their
Icelandic name, are a long strip of 16 islands and numerous
rocks or skerries about 10km (6 miles) off the south coast of
Iceland. Carbon dating has suggested that they may have been
the first part of the country to be inhabited. They were created by underwater eruptions, and the process is still ongoing:
the newest island, Surtsey, emerged from the sea in the mid-
1960s. It has been studied with fascination by scientists, not

just because of its dramatic appearance, but for the flora and fauna that are taking root and making it their home.

The tourist authorities describe the islands as the 'Capri of the North', although even they wouldn't claim it was anything to do with the weather. The coves and inlets may be reminiscent of the chic Italian island, but the rain and wind that batter them for much of the year certainly are not.

HEIMAEY

The only inhabited island is **Heimaey**, which can be reached by ferry (see page 133) or plane, although low cloud can close the airport at short notice. The island has a pretty little town, but most visitors come for the surrounding countryside and **bird cliffs**. Millions of puffins used to come here every year to nest and breed on the precipitous cliffs, although numbers are declining rapidly. You can reach them on foot or take a boat out and get a view from the sea. You might also see whales and seals in the waters around the islands.

The other big draw of Heimaey is the landscape. Two dramatic cones rise up just outside the town: the volcano, Helgafell, and a much newer mountain, Eldfell, created in a massive eruption in 1973 that almost buried the town. In the early hours of 23 January 1973, a fissure nearly 2km (1-mile) long opened up on the eastern side of Helgafell. Red-hot lava started to spurt into the sky, heralding an eruption that was to last for the next six months. The threat to the town was immediate and the entire

Heimaey

The coastline of Surtsey Island, one of the Westman Islands

5,000-strong population was evacuated to the mainland. Flying bombs of molten lava crashed through windows or melted through roofs, and a colossal river of lava made its way towards the town. Many houses collapsed under the weight of falling ash and by the time the flow stopped, a third of Heimaey had been destroyed. When it was all over, the island was 2.2 sq km (0.84 sq miles) larger, and the new mountain of Eldfell had been created. At the edge of the lava, the rather curious Pompeii of the North project has excavated some of the ruined houses on the former street of Suðurvegur. You can learn more about this and other eruptions at the **Eldheimar Museum** (http://eldheimar.is; Wed–Sun mid-Oct–Apr 1–7pm, daily May–mid-Oct 10.30am–6pm).

A walking path runs round the whole island, along some of the best bird cliffs, out to Storhöfði (the island's southernmost tip and the windiest place in Iceland), and back over the new lava to the pretty Skansinn area. Paths also lead to the top of the steep harbourside cliffs – these require careful climbing.

The Westman Islanders are great sports enthusiasts. There are four football fields on the islands and a modern sports centre with a pool. You can easily take in some fishing, horse riding or golf if you stay for long enough.

THE SOUTH COAST

The stretch of highway that runs east along the south of Iceland is a mixture of long, almost featureless lava fields and wonderful views of the mountain and glaciers that come down to the sea in the southeast. It has a reputation as the wettest part of the country, but if the weather holds it is also one of the most dramatic.

As you leave Reykjavík and pass **Selfoss**, heading east, look out for **Mt Hekla**. On a fine day its cone provides a perfect backdrop to Reykjavík, but it's frequently shrouded in

THE PUFFIN POPULATION

The colourful Atlantic puffin – with its large, stripy beak and bright orange legs and feet – is a great favourite with visitors. Puffins are highly sociable, often standing about in groups and nesting in large colonies. They fish together, too, forming wide rafts out to sea. They can dive to 60 metres (200ft) in search of fish, but also eat plankton in winter. They rarely travel far from their colony while raising their young. Both parents incubate a single egg. The males and females look very similar, but neither grow much more than 30cm (12in) in height. The birds are hunted for food in Iceland, fished out of the air with huge nets. They produce a dark meat, like duck but less fatty, often served with a blueberry sauce. However, concerns over declining puffin colonies have led to a hunting ban in the Westman Islands, once the capital of puffin-hunting.

cloud. It is an active volcano that has wiped out farming in the surrounding area several times and erupted every 10 years or so since 1970; however, it can still be climbed fairly easily. Off the ringroad, on Rte 26, the historical (and reputedly haunted) farm of Leirubakki has a small exhibition (tel: 487 8700; www.leirubakki.is; charge) about the volcano.

Millions of Atlantic puffins breed in Iceland

ÞÓRSMÖRK

You are now entering saga country and, in particular, the setting for the bloodiest of the sagas – that which tells the story of the wise and decent Njál and the gruesome end that met most of his friends and family. Much of the action took place at the Alþingi at Þingvellir (see page 41), but there was more than a little blood-letting near the village of Hvolsvöllur, where there is now an Icelandic Saga Centre with background information on the various tales. Here, there is a turning northeast to **Þórsmörk ⑰**, a beautiful nature reserve sheltered between three glaciers. City dwellers from Reykjavík flock here in summer to enjoy mountain walks and lovely views. Note that you have to ford several glacial rivers to get to Þórsmörk, so the route is only open to 4WDs or mountain buses, not ordinary cars.

SKÓGAR

This area sits under Eyjafjallajökull: the 2010 eruptions under the glacier covered everything for miles around in thick grey ash. **Þorvaldseyri visitor centre** (www.icelanderupts.is; June–Aug daily 9am–6pm, May, Sept daily 10am–4pm, Oct–Apr Mon–Fri 11am–4pm) runs a 20-minute film, showing how the farm was affected. 10km (6.2 miles) further east, tiny **Skógar ⑱** is home to a meticulously managed folk museum (www.skogasafn.is; daily June–Aug 9am–6pm, May and Sept 10am–5pm, Oct–Apr 11am–4pm). It contains a 6,000-piece collection and has some fascinating historical buildings in the grounds, including a reconstructed church, a school and a driftwood house.

There is a summer Edda Hotel (www.hoteledda.is) at Skógar, as well as the splendid waterfall, Skógafoss, the sheer fall of which offers one of south Iceland's best photo opportunities. The trek from here to Þórsmörk, passing between the ice-caps of Eyjafjallajökull and Myrdalsjökull over the Fimmvörðuháls pass, is popular with the hardy and becomes

Beautiful scenery around Þórsmörk

quite crowded, particularly in July. There are two huts between the ice-caps: one is an emergency shelter, the other is pre-bookable.

VÍK

Continuing east, the distinctive rock arch at **Dyrhólaey** is a nature reserve packed full of nesting seabirds. The next major stop is the coastal town of **Vík** , or to give its full name, Vík í Mýrdal (Bay of the Marshy Valley). It's a

Skógar homestead

pretty little town, with a beach of black volcanic sand, jagged cliffs and lots of birdlife. Three steeples of stone, known as **Reynisdrangar** (Troll Rocks), rise out of the sea. Legend has it that they are the figures of trolls that turned to stone when they failed to get under cover before the sun hit them. Far more monstrous are the aggressive Arctic terns – Vík contains one of Iceland's largest breeding colonies!

The road crosses more barren fields of lava and *sandur*, a mix of silt, sand and gravel. Oddly shaped boulders are partly overgrown with lichens, helping to give the area a somewhat otherworldly feel. Little wooden bridges cross the rivers, reducing the highway to one lane. In the middle of all this is the tiny hamlet of **Kirkjubæjarklaustur**, a good place to pick up provisions. While doing so, you can reflect on the power of prayer, for it was here that the local pastor delivered his 'Fire Sermon', which believers will tell you halted the flow of lava during the Lakagígar eruption of 1783 and saved the church. A memorial chapel, built in 1974, commemorates the miracle.

Rock formations near Kirkjubæjarklaustur

A rough road, which is accessible only to 4WD vehicles, goes from Kirkjubæjarklaustur to the **Lakagígar Crater Row**, where you can see some of the effects of the 1783 eruptions, which lasted for 10 months and were known as the Skaftáreldar (Skaftá river fires). This was one of the largest effusive eruptions ever recorded, producing about 12 cubic km (2.87 cubic miles). Most of Iceland's livestock died from the poisonous fumes. Some 100 craters extend for 25km (15 miles) up to the glacier; the surrounding lava field is dotted with caves and other lava formations. It takes several hours to see them properly, but there are amazing views from the top of Mt Laki– a climb of about an hour.

VATNAJÖKULL

The massive **Vatnajökull ⓴**, the biggest ice-cap in Europe, is almost 150km (90 miles) across and dominates the southeastern corner of Iceland. Driving around the ring road you can get fascinating glimpses of it as it breaks through the mountains. To get close to the ice-cap, you have to leave the main road and head inland, thought its size and beauty is best appreciated from the air: internal scheduled flights from Reykjavík to Egilsstaðir or Höfn pass close by, or you can take a sightseeing flight from the small airfield at Skaftafell.

In October 1996, the world's media besieged Vatnajökull when a fissure 4km (2.48-miles) long opened beneath the surface of the glacier. Within two days a 10km (6-mile) column of steam was rising above the ice.

Massive flooding was predicted, but the eruption fizzled out, and the journalists departed. Then, on 5 November, the ice dam broke and a huge surge of water burst forth, destroying bridges and roads and carrying massive ice blocks with it.

A number of smaller valley glaciers, all linked to Vatnajökull, are most clearly visible from the road. One of these, Skaftafellsjökull, stops close to **Skaftafell**  (visitor centre; for details check www.vatnajokulsthjodgardur.is), part of Vatnajökull National Park. In the shadow of Iceland's highest peak, **Hvannadalshnúkur** (2,120m/6,950ft), this is serious walking territory and very popular in summer. But with so many trails into the hills, it's not difficult to find solitude.

Hikers take daylong round trips to the higher moorlands and peaks, such as those at **Kristínartindur**. Among the

The glacier lagoon at Jökulsárlón

shorter walks is the route up to **Svartifoss** (Black Falls), named after the surrounding sombre cliffs of basalt, and the wheelchair-accessible path to the edge of the Skaftafellsjökull glacier tongue.

JÖKULSÁRLÓN

Continuing east, the next major point of interest is the extraordinary glacier river lagoon at **Jökulsárlón ㉒**. This photogenic spot is just off the road where a small bridge crosses the mouth of the lake. Great slabs of ice that have broken off the **Breiðamerkurjökull** valley glacier float eerily in the water, some as big as houses. There are around 40 boat cruises daily in summer around Jökulsárlón, weaving among the glistening ice formations.

HÖFN

The final outpost in southeastern Iceland is the town of **Höfn ㉓**, which translates simply as 'harbour'. If you are heading for the Eastfjords (see page 82) by public transport, you might find yourself staying overnight here. It's not the most exciting of places, but it's the largest settlement for miles around. Höfn is famous for its langoustines, and is liveliest during the annual Lobster Festival (Humarhátíð; www.hornafjordur. is), held at the end of June. South of the harbour is Ósland, a promontory with rich birdlife (particularly Arctic tern), from where there are fabulous mountain-and-glacier views. Tours of the icecap by 4WD can be organised from Höfn.

THE NORTH COAST

If you are restricted to just one part of the country in addition to Reykjavík, there is a good chance you will choose the north coast. It's the most accessible region to reach and, in many ways, the liveliest. Akureyri is generally considered to be the capital of the north, and Húsavík is reputedly the best place in Iceland for whale-watching. Despite being close to the Arctic Circle, the north also has the best weather, and temperatures can reach 20°C (68°F) or more in summer. The coastline is very dramatic in places, and there are some huge fjords – a feature that is almost completely lacking in the south.

AKUREYRI

Whether you fly, drive or take a bus you are almost certain to end up in **Akureyri** ㉔. It is an attractive place and has a lot more life about it than most provincial towns. It is home to the only professional theatre in Iceland outside the capital, as well as the only university. Many parts of the country suffer from an exodus of young people, but not Akureyri, which has a youthful feel about it. In summer the town is busy with tourists; in winter it's a major destination for conferences.

Svartifoss, the Black Falls

Akureyri is surrounded by high mountains, which are up to 1,500 metres (5,000ft) tall and snowcapped for much of the year. Green and lush in comparison to many other towns, it even has its own forest, botanical garden and a golf course (every June the Arctic Open tees off under the midnight sun). Akureyri is also a good starting point for visiting some of the most beautiful parts of the country, both to the east and the west.

The centre of town is compact. The main shopping street is the pedestrianised **Hafnarstræti**, where the hustle and bustle (such as it is) of this small town's life takes place. An Akureyri institution, the Bautinn restaurant (www.bautinn.is; tel: 462 1818) at no.92, sits on a crossroads and is a good place to watch the world go by. Hafnarstræti runs from close to the huge main church towards the rather nondescript town square, Ráðhústorg. Running east from the square is Strandgata, which has become the trendy corner of town; this leads down to the

White-tailed ptarmigan, Vatnajökull glacier

port, where cruise liners dock in summer.

The church steeples of the **Akureyrarkirkja** (June–Aug Mon–Thur 10am–7pm, Fri 10am–4pm, Sun 6–8pm, rest of year shorter hours; free) tower over the town and are most dramatic at night when spotlit against the dark sky. The church was designed by the architect Guðjón Samúelsson, who was also responsible for the vast Hallsgrímskirkja in Reykjavík

Akureyrarkirkja

(see page 26). Inside is a fine stained-glass window from the original cathedral at Coventry in the English Midlands. The window was removed at the start of World War II, before the cathedral was destroyed by bombs; it was rescued from a London antiques shop and now forms the centrepiece of an impressive display that also features scenes from Iceland's own history.

Having clambered up to the church, there is a gentler climb to another of the town's main attractions, the **Lystigarðurinn** (Botanical Gardens; Eyrarlandsvegur; www.lystigardur. akureyri.is; June–Sept Mon–Fri 8am–10pm, Sat–Sun 9am–10pm; free). The gardens are famed for their 7,000 species of local and foreign flowers, from southern Europe, Africa, South America and Australasia, all blooming merrily in Akureyri's warm microclimate. The gardens were set up by a local women's association in 1912 to provide a relaxing atmosphere for families. They are very well kept, and are the perfect place to relax on a sunny day: the lovely cafe by the top entrance is open year-round.

Akureyri was the birthplace of the Jesuit priest, Jón Sveinsson, whose children's books were translated into 40 languages. At Aðalstræti 54, you can visit **Nonnahús** (www.nonni.is; June–Aug daily 10am–5pm), the tiny black wooden house where he lived with his widowed mother and five siblings.

Nearby, **Minjasafnið á Akureyri** (Akureyri Municipal Museum; Aðalstræti 58; www.minjasafnid.is; June–mid-Sept daily 9am–5pm, mid-Sept–May daily 1–4pm) has a wide collection of everyday items that date as far back as the settlement in the 9th century, including a beautifully painted pulpit. The church here is still used for weddings. **Listasafnið á Akureyri** (Kaupvangsstræti 12; www.listak.is; daily June–Aug 10am–5pm; free, Sept–May Tue–Sun noon–5pm) is the town's **Art Museum** and offers visitors one of the best insights into the town's present-day cultural life.

The Botanical Gardens

The town's **swimming pool** (Þingvallastræti 2; tel: 461 4455; Mon–Fri 6.45am–9pm, Sat & Sun 9am–6.30pm) is one of the best in the country, with two outdoor pools, an indoor pool, two waterslides, hot tubs, a steam room and sauna. In summer, there are extra distractions for children, including mini-golf and electric cars.

An hour's walk south of the town is one of Iceland's few wooded areas at **Kjarnaskógur**. Given the shortage of trees in Iceland, this is considered something of an attraction, and the townspeople flock here on sunny weekends. There is a children's play area, picnic sites and a jogging track.

EYJAFJÖRÐUR

From Akureyri two roads fork off to the north along each side of Eyjafjörður fjord. The cluster of towns and villages on the banks of the fjord are hemmed in close to the water by high mountains. The land here is particularly fertile, and the mild climate makes it good farming territory. It is a suitable area for exploring both on land and at sea, with ferry links to the islands of Grímsey and Hrísey.

Dalvík, a fishing village about an hour's drive north of Akureyri, was rebuilt after an earthquake in 1934 demolished half its buildings, but the harbour front is still attractive. The town has a good outdoor swimming pool and an interesting museum, **Byggðasafnið Hvoll** (Karlsbraut; www.dalvi kurbyggd.is/byggdasafn; June–Aug daily 11am–6pm, Sept–May Sat 2–5pm and by previous arrangement), which contains photographs of Iceland's tallest man, Jóhann Kristinn Pétursson (see box) and many of his possessions.

The main reason that people come to Dalvík is to catch the ferry to the island of **Grímsey ㉕**. The Arctic Circle runs through the centre of this island: once you've crossed it, you can buy yourself a commemorative certificate from the local cafe. The

Big in Iceland

Iceland's tallest man, Jóhann Kristinn Pétursson, known as Jóhann the Giant, was an impressive 2.34 metres (7ft 8in) tall. Born in 1913, he worked in circuses and shows across Europe and the United States. He returned to Dalvík late in his life and died there in 1984.

small settlement of **Sandvík** has some basic services, including a swimming pool. The community centre commemorates the island's benefactor, Daniel Willard Fiske, a 19th-century American chess champion who had read about its reputation for producing great chess players since Viking days. He left money for a school and library to be built and donated 11 marble chessboards. The locals still celebrate his birthday on 11 November although hardly any of them play chess any more.

Grímsey is well known for its extensive **birdlife** – the craggy cliffs on the north and east of the island are home to about 60 species, including puffins, kittiwakes and razorbills. You can explore on your own or find a local guide in the town. The only proper road runs along the west side of Grímsey from Sandvík to the airport, from where there are regular flights to Akureyri. The runway has to be regularly cleared of birds, and this is sometimes done by incoming flights buzzing the airstrip before coming round again to land.

The Dalvík–Grímsey ferry stops at the island of **Hrísey**; there is also a far more frequent service from Árskógssandur, just south of Dalvík, departing every two hours in summer. Iceland's second-largest island is another choice destination for bird lovers. It is particularly famous for its fearless ptarmigan; they are prolific all year round, although their number swells in the autumn, and they can often be seen waddling down the streets. There are around 40 species of birds on the island, and it is an important breeding ground for eider ducks and Arctic tern.

On the eastern side of the fjord the first place of interest is the fishing village of **Svalbarðseyri**. According to local folklore, this is home to a large community of elves who live in the cliffs behind the village. Even if this sounds all rather unlikely, you are still sure to be enchanted here by the rugged coastline.

At **Laufás**, around 30km (19 miles) north of Akureyri, there is a magnificent example of a 19th-century turf farmhouse, maintained by Akureyri Museum (June–mid-Sept daily 9am–5pm). Inside there is a multitude of effects showing how life was lived here more than 100 years ago. The timber church dates from 1865.

WEST OF AKUREYRI

On the route west, the tiny village of **Hofsós** is home to **Vesturfarasetrið** (Icelandic Emigration Centre; http://en.hofsos.is; June–Aug daily 11am–6pm). If you think you are of

Laufás turf farmhouse

Icelandic descent, this is the place to come to try to trace your roots. It is not just for genealogists, though – there is a great exhibition telling the story of those Icelanders who emigrated west to the New World. A small but astonishing outdoor **swimming pool** (www.facebook.com/sundlaugin hofsosi; Mon–Fri 7am–1pm, 5–8pm, Sat–Sun 11am–3pm) in Hofsós overlooks the fjord: it's not uncommon to see whales swim past as you're doing your lengths.

Hólar í Hjaltadal, 25km (15 miles) southeast and inland from the coast road, was once a thriving cultural and religious centre. Until the Reformation, it was a great seat of learning, with monks studying the scriptures and transcribing manuscripts. It housed the country's first printing press, dating from 1530. A red-stone **cathedral** (mid-May–Aug daily 10am–6pm), dating from 1759–63, commemorates its religious past. There is sacred art and sculpture on display, as well as a modern

Exterior of Hólar cathedral

mosaic by the artist Erró. The bones of the last Catholic bishop in Iceland, Jón Arason, are buried here. He was beheaded in 1550 for resisting the spread of the protestant Reformation. In summer, classical concerts are held here.

Another important historical site is **Þingeyrar**, 85km (53 miles) further west. It was the home of one of the first regional assemblies, as well as the first monastery in 1133. It was here that many of the sagas were first written, and other texts were transcribed by the monks. The monastery disappeared after the Reformation, but there is an impressive 19th-century church, **Þingeyrarkirkja** (June–early Sept daily 10am–6pm), made of basalt, that is visible for miles around. The interior has white walls, green pews and a dramatic blue ceiling painted with 1,000 gold stars. The altarpiece, which was made in Nottingham, England, came from the old monastery.

HÚSAVÍK

To the northeast of Akureyri, **Húsavík** ㉖ occupies a beautiful setting, facing the Víknafjöll mountains over the wide waters of Skjálfandi ('Trembling Bay'). Unsurprisingly, the sea has always been a dominant factor in the town's development, and today people flock here for **whale-watching tours**, for which Húsavík is renowned. The two big operators, North Sailing (tel: 464 7272; www.northsailing.is) and Gentle Giants (tel: 464 1500; www.gentlegiants.is) have between one and 12 sailings per day between April and November: buy tickets from the harbourside huts. In breeding season, they also run trips to two small islands, Lundey and Flatey, to look at puffins.

Down at the harbour is the excellent **Húsavík Whale Museum** (www.whalemuseum.is; May–Sept daily 8.30am– 6.30pm, weekdays Oct–Apr 9am–2pm), Iceland's only museum dedicated to these captivating mammals. It is small, but packed with information to help explain the life-cycle, habits and biology of whales. The highlight is the long gallery, where skeletons of whales swim eerily overhead.

Húsavík also has a fine natural history museum, **Safnahúsið** (www.husmus.is; Stórigarður 17; June–Aug daily 10am–6pm, Sept–May Mon–Fri 10am–4pm), in the

WHALES AND WHALING

For many visitors, Iceland's attitude to whaling is perplexing. The country has an excellent record for environmental protection and an apparent deep respect for nature. Nevertheless, whaling is a topic that continues to arouse passionate nationalistic feelings in Iceland, with polls indicating widespread popular support for the commercial hunt.

The abundance of whales off Iceland's coasts inevitably led to them being caught and killed for food. In 1948 this developed into a commercial whaling industry that continued until 1989, when strong international pressure led to a break in whaling.

In 2003, Iceland announced its intention to begin 'scientific' whaling; and in 2006 it once again resumed the commercial hunt. To many outside observers, this decision might have appeared self-defeating. However, in spite of these fears, tourist numbers have risen steadily since 2006.

Still, Icelandic whaling is a strange kettle of fish. Only around five percent of Icelanders eat whale regularly: tourists are now its main devourers within the domestic market. The rest, including meat from endangered fin whales, is exported to Japan, for human consumption and for luxury dog treats. The Icelandic government stresses that whale-hunting quotas (229 minke and 154 fin whales for the 2015/2016 seasons) are "well within the generally accepted values for sustainable catch rates of whale stocks". However, difficulties in exporting the whale meat to the Japanese market lead the Icelandic whaling company, Hvalur, to cancel the hunt for endangered animals in summer 2016.

same building as the town library. As well as memorabilia from old houses and farms, various old weapons and exhibits of flora and fauna (including a stuffed polar bear captured on the island of Grímsey in 1969), there is a beautifully displayed maritime section that reflects the town's historical dependence on the sea.

Whale-watching

The **church** (Garðarsbraut; daily June–Aug 9–11am, 3–5pm), an impressive wooden building in the shape of a cross, was built in 1906–7 to seat 450 people. The altarpiece features several of the town's residents who posed for a depiction of the resurrection of Lazarus. East of Húsavík, **Þórshöfn** is another place that dates back to the saga times. It grew considerably in the early 20th century during the peak of the herring boom and is still predominantly a fishing town.

Britain's Prince Charles used to favour **Vopnafjörður**, 60km (37 miles) to the southeast, for fishing holidays. He must have arrived by air, as the roads around here are among the worst in Iceland. The locals will tell you that Santa Claus lives on the nearby **Smjörfjöll** – at least he is able to travel freely by sleigh.

LAKES, VOLCANOES, CANYONS AND FALLS

Within easy striking distance of both Akureyri and Húsavík are some of the most impressive geological formations in Iceland. These include two massive waterfalls, Dettifoss and Goðafoss, and Jökulsárgljúfur (see page 79), part of Vatnajökull National Park, which encloses a spectacular canyon with falls of its own. Active geothermal areas, craters and bizarre rock formations surround Lake Mývatn, home to a huge variety of ducks. A good road circles the lake close to the shore.

The perfectly proportioned falls at **Goðafoss** ㉗ are easily reached on the drive into the area from the north. The 'Waterfall of the Gods' was so-named because, after returning in the year 1000 from the momentous Alþingi, where he had decided that Iceland should convert to Christianity, lawspeaker Þorgeir threw his pagan carvings into its waters.

LAKE MÝVATN

Despite its name, **Lake Mývatn** ㉘ (Midge Lake) is one of the highlights of any visit to Iceland. Midges and flies love the shallow water at the lake's edge, but they rarely bite, and you can get a hat with netting attached to keep them out of eyes, ears and mouth. The lake, and the **Laxá River** that flows out from

The falls at Goðafoss

the west, are renowned for the variety of **birds** they attract. The area is protected by law, and there are wardens to help visitors enjoy themselves without harming the ecology.

With the peaks of the Krafla caldera and Mt Hverfjall as a backdrop, Lake Mývatn has a serenity that belies the churning geothermal activity just below the surface of the sur-

Húsavík harbour

rounding land. The land around the shore is generally flat, with just a few small hills and pseudocraters, making it ideal territory for gentle hiking or cycling. The Environment Agency of Iceland (www.ust.is/the-environment-agency-of-iceland) publishes a list of suggested trails. It is worth carrying binoculars because, whether you are an avid birdwatcher or not, the number and variety of ducks and other birdlife here is extraordinary (see box).

Tiny **Reykjahlíð** at the northeast corner of Lake Mývatn has the most amenities, including the tourist office, which can arrange all manner of tours, and a small supermarket. The main sight in the village is its **church**, which is surrounded by hardened lava. A major eruption in 1729 brought lava streaming down from the hills. While it obliterated nearby farmland, it miraculously skirted around the church. Tradition says it was the power of prayer that protected it, although the walls around the cemetery may have helped.

There is plenty of evidence to indicate just how close the geothermal activity is to the surface in this part of Iceland – you may well see gases rising from fissures in the lava around Reykjahlíð. Heading clockwise around the lake, you can sample geothermally-baked *hverabrauð* (see box) at the popular Cowshed Café (Vogafjós; www.vogafjos.is; daily 10am–10.30pm), which backs onto a milking shed, so you can watch the working life of the farm while you eat. Slightly set back from the shore road, the hot springs at **Storagjá** can be reached via a ladder and rope. The springs have cooled and become infested with algae, which dissuades most potential swimmers. Nearby, another spring **Grjótagjá** suffers from the opposite problem – it is too hot for most people, but is well

THE DUCKS AND BIRDS OF MÝVATN

Fourteen species of ducks breed on Lake Mývatn and the Laxá River at a density unmatched anywhere else in the world. There are tens of thousands of these birds, all attracted by the warm shallow water, plentiful food and space for nesting.

The most common varieties are the tufted duck, scaup, wigeon, teal and red-breasted merganser. Harlequin ducks live on the river in large numbers, and the common scoter, a diving breed, is widely seen on the west side of the lake. Barrow's goldeneye is only found here and in North America. In the Rockies, where the species originates, the birds lay their eggs in holes in tree trunks; here, they lay them in holes in the lava. The Slavonian grebe builds floating nests close to the shore. The gadwall and red-necked phalarope are common all over the lake.

Other breeds you are likely to see include whooper swans, greylag geese, Arctic tern and the black-headed gull. Ptarmigan are common, and there are several pairs of gyrfalcon nesting here, along with smaller numbers of short-eared owl and merlin.

Sigurgeirs Bird Museum (Fuglasafn Sigurgeirs; www.fuglasafn.is; tel: 464 4477; daily June–Aug 9am–6pm, Sept–Oct noon–5pm, Nov–mid-May 2–4pm), on Neslandatangi peninsula in the northwestern part of the lake, is great for twitchers. It contains stuffed examples of most Icelandic birds, and has bookable hides at the heart of the action.

worth a look as it's inside a naturally formed cavern in the lava.

Skirting the edge of the vast tephra cone Hverfjall is enchanting **Dimmuborgir**, a vast, 2,000-year-old field of contorted volcanic pillars, some extending as high as 20 metres (65ft). The helpful visitor centre and café (June–Aug daily 9am–10pm, reduced hours Apr–May, Sept–Dec) offers guided walks in the area. A viewing platform looks

Lake Mývatn

out over the expanse, and visitors can wander among haunting arches, caves and natural tunnels – stick to the paths, as the area is very fragile. The most famous formation is Kirkjan (the Church), a cave whose entrance looks like the window of a Gothic cathedral.

At the southern end of the lake, **Skútustaðir** has a hotel, church, café-restaurant and facilities for horse riding and hiring bikes. Close to the shore there is a collection of pseudocraters, which look like mini volcanoes. In fact they were created when molten lava ran over the marshland. The water below came to the boil and burst through the lava sheet to form cones. Most of the islands in the middle of the lake were formed in the same way.

The Laxá River contains salmon, brown trout and Arctic char, but you'll need to buy an expensive licence if you want to fish. On the eastern side of the lake is the peak of **Vindbelgjarfjall** (530 metres/1,735ft), which can be climbed by a fairly steep path at the back of the mountain for some fantastic views. From here, the road passes through wetlands containing some of the biggest concentrations of birdlife, before returning to Reykjahlíð.

NÁMAFJALL AND KRAFLA

The geothermal sights northeast of the lake are ever more amazing. Four kilometres east of Reykjahlíð are the **Mývatn Nature Baths** (Jarðböðin; www.myvatnnaturebaths.is; daily summer 9am–midnight, winter noon–10pm), the north's answer to the Blue Lagoon, though without the crowds. The pool covers 5,000 sq metres (5,980 sq yds) and contains a mix of skin-softening minerals, silicates and micro-organisms. It is the perfect place to sit and soak for an hour or two.

The baths are filled with geothermally heated water from the Bjarnarflag borehole, which taps into a nearby geothermal field. You can admire the sulphurous earth, bubbling mudpots and screaming fumaroles of this high-temperature area at the unearthly Hverir, a little further along the ringroad from the baths.

Just past Hverir, road 863 branches north towards the **Krafla caldera** ㉙. There have been eruptions in and around Krafla for much of the past 3,000 years. Nine eruptions between 1977–84 (the so-called Krafla Fires) left a huge field of lava that is still steaming today. The eruptions threatened the **Leirbotn power station**, but stopped just short; you can visit the plant for free most afternoons. Further up the road is a perfectly rounded crater **Viti** ('Hell'), which was formed in 1724 and has since flooded. Its huge size, the strange blue tint to the water

Daily bread

The local tradition of underground baking involves mixing rye dough with yeast and molasses, pouring the mixture into old milk cartons and baking them in holes covered by metal sheets for a day. The result is a heavy but moist steam bread known as *hverabrauð*.

The Grjótagjá pool

and the sheer drop down from the rim makes it an awesome sight. From the Krafla car park you can visit a second crater, **Sjálfskapar Viti**, or 'Home-made Hell', so-called because it was formed when a borehole being drilled for the power station exploded. Fortunately, nobody was killed, but debris from the rig was found for miles around. A well-marked track leads up to the **Leirhnjúkur** lavafield, formed in the mid-18th century and provoked back to life by the Krafla Fires. The path leads past a large and colourful sulphur-encrusted mud-hole, before winding its way around an area of cinder-like mounds and smoking black fissures. Stick to the well-worn paths, for this fragile area's safety and your own: the crust is thin and could give way under a person's weight.

JÖKULSÁRGLJÚFUR

North of Mývatn, **Jökulsárgljúfur**, part of Vatnajökull National Park, straddles part of Iceland's second-longest river, the **Jökulsá á Fjöllum**. More than half the country's plant species are to be found here, but most visitors are drawn by the geology of the area.

Jökulsárgljúfur ('glacier river canyon') is a vast canyon up to 120 metres (395ft) deep and 500 metres (1,640ft) wide. There are numerous waterfalls along its route. The two most impressive, **Dettifoss** (Europe's most powerful falls) and **Selfoss**, are situated at the southern boundary of the park. At the northern tip is the information office where you can acquire details of the area's many walking trails and sights.

From the tourist office, a road leads down towards the great horse-shoe shaped **Ásbyrgi canyon**, a 90 metre (295ft) semicircle of rock flecked with colourful lichens. The first Viking settlers believed that Sleipnir, the god Odin's flying horse, formed the canyon by crashing a giant hoof into the earth. There are several campsites in the park if you want to stay and explore the area.

EASTERN ICELAND

The eastern part of Iceland is one of the least-visited areas of the country and, as a result, has a less well-developed tourist industry. Overall, the region has a quiet, gentle feel, making it pleasant to visit. The East enjoys some of the sunniest weather in the country – and the undulating farmland and rugged coast are ideal for walking.

For the past decade, the region has been at the centre of the greatest environmental debate Iceland has ever known, when it was chosen as the site for an immense dam and aluminium smelter. Construction on the smelter began in

Reyðarfjörður in 2004, and was completed by 2008. It transformed the local economy and created scores of new jobs, yet its power is supplied by the Kárahnjúkar Dam, which was built in an environmentally sensitive part of the interior.

EGILSSTAÐIR

With its airport and its pivotal position on the ring road, **Egilsstaðir ③** is the most-visited town in the region. It is not the loveliest of places, but it's a good base for trips to the lakes and mountains to the south of it. A regional museum, **Minjasafn Austurlands** (East Iceland Heritage Museum, Tjarnabraut; www.minjasafn.is; June–Aug Mon–Fri 11.30am– 7pm, Sat–Sun10.30am–6pm, Sept–May Tue–Fri 11am–4pm), contains exhibits about life in the area. At the northern end of the town is a 25-metre **swimming pool**, which is ideal for relaxing in after a day's walking.

Ásbyrgi canyon

Snake charm
According to folklore, a young girl found a gold ring and put it in a box with a small snake for safekeeping. When she returned, both the ring and snake had grown. Terrified, she threw them into Lögurinn. The snake grew into the Lagarfljótsormur monster, threatening all who crossed the lake.

LÖGURINN AND SNÆFELL

The lake of **Lögurinn** runs 30km (19 miles) south from Egilsstaðir, carrying the **Lagarfljót River** from the Vatnajökull ice cap to the sea. The road around it is rough in places, but, unusually for Iceland, the banks are forested, especially over on the eastern side. The lake is in a deep glacial valley and is said to be home to the **Lagarfljótsormur monster**, a creature not unlike Scotland's Loch Ness monster, although nobody seems to have got close enough to be sure.

The forest at **Hallormsstaður** is the showcase for Iceland's efforts at reforestation after the indiscriminate felling of previous eras. The **arboretum** has examples of around 70 tree species from around the world, all of which are well labelled. There are marked trails here for hikes or horseriding.

At 1,833 metres (6,012ft), **Mt Snæfell ③** is Iceland's highest peak outside the glacial zones. An ancient volcano, Snæfell last erupted some 10,000 years ago. There are marker posts up the western side of the mountain showing the easiest route to the top, although you need to be experienced to tackle the peak itself. However, there are plenty of easier walks on the mountain, and there is the added attraction of the many reindeer that inhabit the area.

THE EASTFJORDS

Although the inlets along the east of Iceland are less dramatic than those in the west and north, they are dotted with lovely little villages, most of which are easily accessible from the ring road. Travellers arriving in Iceland by ferry normally dock at **Seyðisfjörður** , a pretty little port surrounded by high mountains. A dirt road up to Mt Bjólfur gives spectacular views down over the fjord and the town's brightly painted wooden houses. Although just 665 people live here, Seyðisfjörður has a healthy cultural life: Skaftfell Culture Center stages contemporary art exhibitions; **Bláa kirkjan** (The Blue Church) organises classical concerts on Wednesday evenings from July to mid-August. The town commissioned the unusual sculpture Tvísöngur, perched high in the hills and worth the walk. At the mouth of the 20km (12.42-mile) long fjord, the nature reserve Skálanes (www.skalanes.com), accessible only by boat, on foot or in a 4WD, provides an end-of-the-earth retreat.

In summer, boats (Flóabáturinn Anný; tel: 476 0005 or 853 3004) sail from **Neskaupstaður** around the headland into near-deserted **Mjóifjörður**, past the highest sea-cliff in Iceland.

Seyðisfjörður is surrounded by mountains

Eskifjörður is a busy fishing village with a large trawler fleet and a fish-freezing plant. **Sjóminjasafn** (Maritime Museum; Strandgata 39b; June–Aug daily 2–5pm) is packed with boats, models, nets and fishing equipment. Just south of here, easy walking paths run through the **Hólmanes nature reserve**. It lies at the foot of the **Hólmatindur** headland, whose summit makes a more challenging climb.

The hills around the small fishing port of **Reyðarfjörður** have been worn flat by the now-vanished glaciers. The town was a naval base during World War II, and there is a museum, **Stríðsárasafnið** (Icelandic Wartime Museum, Austurvegur; June–Aug daily 1–5pm), which documents the billeting of 3,000 Allied soldiers here.

A river running through Hallormsstaður forest

A trip out from **Djúpivogur** to the uninhabited island of **Papey**, 'Monk's Island', reveals Iceland's smallest church, little bigger than a hencoop, which is chained to the ground to prevent it blowing away. Today the island is a nature reserve, home to seabirds (including 30,000 puffin pairs) and a large breeding colony of eider ducks.

THE INTERIOR

Iceland's barren interior – a place so desolate that the Apollo astronauts came here to train for their moon landing – can be crossed by two main north–south routes; Sprengisandur (F26) and Kjölur (F35, also known as the Kjalvegur), both of which are open only once the snow has melted in summer. Some of the more minor routes remain closed throughout the summer if conditions are poor. East of Mývatn, the F88 eventually splits into several highland 'dead-ends': however, the final destinations – the distinctive mountain Herðubreið,

Kids at Lögurinn lake

the Askja caldera and the Kverkfjöll ice caves – are stunning. The weather is generally very unpredictable in the interior, so always be prepared for the worst.

Camping is the only form of accommodation, apart from a few huts operated by Ferðafélag Íslands (Iceland Touring Association; tel: 568 2533; www.fi.is), plus the Hrauneyjar motel (www.hrauneyjar.is) and Kiðagil guesthouse (www.kidagil.is) at either end of the Sprengisandur route. Visitors without transport can take advantage of the scheduled buses that run between Reykjavík and Lake Mývatn via Sprengisandur (late-June–Aug three times weekly) and between Reykjavík and Akureyri via the Kjölur route (late-June–early Sept daily). Private tour operators can take you from Akureyri and Mývatn to Herðubreið, Askja and Kverkfjöll.

ASKJA AND HERÐUBREIÐ

From Mývatn, the F88 crosses a moonlike plateau and several glacial streams before reaching the distinctive table mountain Herðubreið, known as the queen of Iceland's mountains, and the flower-filled nature reserve Herðubreiðarlindir. The F88 turns into the F910, with one branch bumping on to the stunning **Askja caldera** ⊕, the scene of epic eruptions in 1874–5 when vents under lake Öskjuvatn threw out two billion cubic metres of ash. On the edge of the lake, the crater Víti (Hell) contains milky-blue water that is still warm from the last eruption in 1961 – bring a swimsuit. The other branch heads south, eventually petering out at the mighty icecap Vatnajökull: a steep hike brings you to spectacular ice caves inside the Kverkfjöll glacier. Further south is the **Holuhraun lava field**, a new attraction that was formed during an eruption of the Bardarbunga volcano, which lasted from August 2014 to February 2015.

THE SPRENGISANDUR ROUTE

The second main crossing through the interior, the Sprengisandur route, runs from the Bárðardalur Valley between

Landmannalaugar's rhyolitic hills

Akureyri and Lake Mývatn to Þjórsá, east of Selfoss. It is accessible by 4WD only and covers some of the most desolate ground in the country.

Campsite at Landmannalaugar

There are three main ways to reach the start of the route proper, all of which converge at or near Laugafell at the edge of the Sprengisandur. The most easterly way (route 842 then F26) heads through the Bárðardalur Valley via two waterfalls; Goðafoss and the basalt Aldeyjarfoss. A more central route (F821) goes from the end of the Eyjafjörður Valley, past the former farm/weather station at Nýibær, towards Laugafell. The third, most westerly, route (F752) meanders through the Vesturdalur Valley from Skagafjörður.

At Laugafell, on a ridge leading northwest from the mountain of the same name, there are several warm springs, a warm bathing pool and a tourist hut. Nearby, the gravel expanse of the Sprengisandur begins with magnificent vistas east to Vatnajökull and the smaller Tungnafellsjökull and west to Hofsjökull. A number of river crossings later, the blue tongues of glaciers come into view.

At Nýidalur, close to the geographical centre of Iceland, is a small campsite, on the only patch of green in the area, and several huts. The next stop on the route is shortly after the mountain of Kistualda (790m/2,600ft). The dusty track south to **Þórisvatn ㉞**, Iceland's second largest lake, continues the landscape of glaciers and black gravel plains. Just beyond the lake is the tiny settlement of Hrauneyjafoss, where there is

Bathing in natural hot springs

a petrol station, coffee-shop and small guesthouse.

Next is **Landmannalaugar** ㉟, part of the Fjallabak Nature Reserve and a good base for the many walks in the area (there are camping and hut facilities here). Landmannalaugar's spectacular rhyolitic hills are bright yellow, green and red, dotted with deep blue lakes. There are hot springs here, and steam rises from every corner of the valley.

From Landmannalaugar, it is possible either to head south-westwards to meet the ring road near the south coast, or southeast to Bláfjall and the coast.

THE KJÖLUR ROUTE

Comparatively straightforward to drive, the Kjölur is the most popular crossing through the central highlands. This is the only route through the interior that travellers could consider making in a normal car, as all the rivers are bridged. However, rental cars are not insured for the route; and it is still strongly advised to travel by 4WD.

Based on an ancient byway used in saga times, the route runs from Gullfoss to the Blöndudalur Valley, passing between the Langjökull and Hofsjökull ice-caps. Behind Gullfoss, the River Hvítá flows out of Hvítárvatn, a glacial lake at the foot of Langjökull. From the main route you should be able to see the lake and its glacial spurs, which extend up to its shores.

The route soon reaches its highest point (just over 670 metres/2,200ft), where a memorial stone commemorates the achievements of Geir Zoëga, an engineer who was for many years in charge of building Iceland's roads.

At the centre of the Kjölur plateau is **Hveravellir** , an area of intense geothermal activity, with hot springs, a hot pool where you can bathe, camping facilities and good overnight huts. Also at Hveravellir is a modest stone shelter where the bandit Fjalla Eyvindur and his wife Halla spent a whole winter in hiding in the 18th century.

The northern section of the route, which is less attractive, follows a track through the reservoir basin created for Blönduvirkjun hydroelectric power station. After crossing the Blandá River at about halfway between Blönduós and Varmahlíð, you will reach the Blöndudalur Valley and then the ring road.

Geothermal spring at Hveravellir

WHAT TO DO

OUTDOOR ACTIVITIES

There is a great deal on offer for exploring the great outdoors in Iceland, from gentle hikes and horse-riding excursions to more demanding pursuits such as ice-climbing and white-water rafting.

WALKING AND HIKING

There are hiking trails throughout Iceland to suit every level. The more ambitious routes require some previous experience and a high level of fitness. The weather can change unexpectedly and if you can't read a map and a compass properly then don't attempt the hikes that take you away from populated areas.

The two organisations that provide hiking information, details of mountain huts for overnight stays, as well as guided hikes are: **Ferðafélag Íslands** (Iceland Touring Association, Mörkin 6, 108 Reykjavík, tel: 568 2533, www.fi.is) and **Útivist** (Laugavegur 178, 105 Reykjavík, tel: 562 1000, www.utivist.is). Tourist offices can provide maps and local contacts for guides.

By far the best months for hiking are June, July and August, when the weather is relatively warm, and visibility is at its best. Beginners could start with some of the excellent walking paths around Reykjavík: the longest runs right round the headland, passing Grótta lighthouse, Seltjarnarnes golf club and Nauthólsvík geothermal beach, before heading 10km (6 miles) east inland to the Heiðmörk conservation area. Ask the tourist office for further information.

Every part of the country has its trails. Some of the best areas for walking and hiking include:

Þingvellir National Park. Marked trails around historic sites and lakes. One option is a full-day hike up Mt Armannsfell.

Enjoying the water in the Eastfjords

Landmannalaugar–Þórsmörk Trail. Experienced walkers will love Iceland's best-known hike, the 53km (33 miles) 'Laugavegurinn'. It can be extended to reach Skógar, a further 25km (15.5 miles) to the south.

Snæfellsnes Peninsula. A rugged and often wet area. Ascent of the glacier for experienced hikers.

Hornstrandir. One of the wildest and most isolated parts of the country, suitable for the experienced only.

Lake Mývatn. Flat and gentle routes amid terrific scenery.

Jökulsárgljúfur (Vatnajökull National Park). Well-marked trails at all levels, taking from a few hours to four days.

Skaftafell (Vatnajökull National Park). Trails at different levels, from a well-trodden glacier path to the unmarked 24km (15-mile) round-trip to Kjós.

Mt Snæfell. Demanding hikes from Egilsstaðir along the lake and up the mountain. An 80km (50-mile) trail runs from Snæfell to Stafafell, in the Lónsöræfi wilderness area.

Hikes into the **interior**, where there are few roads and no villages, can be very tough but rewarding. The mighty rivers make many of the routes and tracks impassable by foot, but the **F35 Kjölur track** is passable in summer without a vehicle. Always seek advice from one of the touring organisations (see page 91) before setting off.

HORSE RIDING

Icelandic horses are descended from the sturdy breed brought over by the Vikings. They can be hired, with or without guides, from farms and activity centres all over Iceland. Treks can be as short as an hour, or as long as 10 days, with accommodation in tents or huts. If you are bringing your own equipment or clothing it must be disinfected on arrival. Contact local tourist offices for details of tour providers, or see the Icelandic Farm Holidays website (www.farmholidays.

Spectacular hiking country

is) for a list of farms offering horse-riding tours and holidays. The magazine *Eíðfaxi International* (http://en.eidfaxi.is) is published for Icelandic horse lovers worldwide.

FISHING

Salmon and trout fishing in Iceland have an international reputation. For salmon, the season is from the third week of May until mid-September, with fishing permitted for 105 days within that period; and for trout it's April/May until late September/October, depending on the location. Excellent fishing is available but at a very high price, which varies according to river and facilities available. The very cheapest salmon permits start at around ISK40,000 per rod per day in peak season, usually as part of a (minimum) three-day package. The other snag is that most rivers have to be booked months, if not years, in advance. Iceland's waters are disease-free, so all equipment coming into the country, including waders and boots, must be disinfected. For

Ice-climbing

further information contact the **Federation of Icelandic River Owners** (Bændahöllin, Hagatorg, 107 Reykjavík, tel: 563 0300, www.angling.is).

Sea angling has traditionally been considered an industry rather than a pastime, but it is now becoming popular as a sport, with catfish, cod, haddock and halibut the most frequent catches. The season begins in late May and runs until the end of August. Trips are best arranged directly through hotels and farms on the coast.

BIRDWATCHING

The quantity and variety of bird life in Iceland really has to be seen to be believed: the country is home to some of the largest breeding colonies in the world. The best locations are:
Látrabjarg in the West Fjords: the largest bird cliff in Europe.
Heimaey: once the site of Iceland's largest puffin colony, although numbers are in sharp decline. Other puffin-packed places include Lundey Island near Reykjavík; around the cliffs at Vík; at Borgarfjörður Eystri.
Lake Mývatn, in the north: there are more species of breeding ducks here than anywhere in Europe.
Dyrhólaey Cliffs and elsewhere along the south coast has Arctic tern as well as the world's largest skua colony.
The **Icelandic Society for the Protection of Birds (Fuglaverndarfélag Íslands)** can be contacted at Hverfisgötu 105, 101 Reykjavik, tel: 562 0477, http://fuglavernd.is.

ICE-CLIMBING AND GLACIER WALKS

In summer, guided day-walks on the glaciers from Skaftafell (part of Vatnajökull National Park) can be arranged with two companies based at the visitor centre; the **Icelandic Mountain Guides** (tel: 587 9999, www.mountainguide.is) and the **Glacier Guides** (tel: 659 7000, 571 2100, www.glacier guides.is). **Ice Guide** (tel: 894 1317, www.localguide.is) offers private tours on various glaciers within the national park. They and the Icelandic Mountain Guides also offer more ambitious winter expeditions, including ice climbing and ascents of Iceland's highest peak Hvannadalshnúkur – see the websites for details.

ICELAND'S BIRDLIFE

Iceland is renowned for its birdlife, hosting around 270 (mostly migratory) species. Sea-birds make up the majority – some of the world's largest breeding colonies of gannets, guillemots, razorbills, storm-petrels, arctic skuas, arctic terns and puffins are found here – although there has been a worrying crash in the number of breeding pairs. There are also large numbers of waders and wildfowl. Many species are strictly protected by law.

The lesser black-backed gull is the first migrant to arrive, in February/March, but the locals regard the arrival of the golden plover in April as the start of spring. The best time to go birdwatching is in early summer. Many breeds pass through during the last two weeks of May on their way north to Greenland. In early June the resident breeding species begin their mating rituals. It is important not to disturb the birds at this time. In the second half of June the chicks start to hatch and by mid-August they are leaving the nest. While a few breeds migrate to Iceland for the winter, there is not much to see and puffins, for example, will have gone in search of warmer climes.

Glacier tours with **snowmobiles** are a fun (if noisy!) way to see the ice close up. Several companies run trips on to the Vatnajökull glacier in the southeast, Snæfellsjökull in the west, and Langjökull in the southwest, close to the sights of the Golden Circle. Contact local tourist offices for details.

SNOW SPORTS

You probably wouldn't come to Iceland just for the **downhill skiing** and **snowboarding**, although they are popular diversions for Icelanders making the best of the dark northern winter. On clear, calm weekends in March and April, the whole of Reykjavík seems to head out of town to the Bláfjöll skiing area (tel: 530 3000; www.skidasvaedi.is), where there are 15 busy lifts and a cafe. A day pass costs a very reasonable ISK3,400, boot and ski hire ISK5,000, and the lifts are open Mon–Fri 2–9pm and weekends 10am–5pm. Scheduled buses depart from the Mjódd bus terminal on the eastern outskirts of Reykjavík once a day. There are also good slopes at Akureyri (tel: 462 2280, www.hlidarfjall.is).

Several tour operators run **cross-country skiing** trips in spring: check with Ferðafélag and Útivist (see page 91), or with Ice Guide and the Icelandic Mountain Guides (see page 95).

Speeding on the Skálafellsjökull

Dog-sledding Iceland (tel: 863 6733, www.dogsledding.is) run excursions on Langjökull glacier in the southwest, snow conditions permitting.

WHITE-WATER RAFTING

Visitors can shoot the rapids on three of Iceland's glacial

Iceland offers great opportunities for whale-watching

rivers between May and mid-September. The fairly gentle Hvítá river is easily accessed on day trips from Reykjavík. However, if you're heading north, the remote Jökulsá Vestari and Jökulsá Austari, near Varmahlíð in Skagafjörður, should be your first choice. The western branch is suitable for families, while the eastern river is a wilder ride. For details (including minimum ages), contact Arctic Rafting, (tel: 562 7000, www.arcticrafting.com).

SWIMMING

More than just a sport in Iceland, swimming is a social activity for all the family, and there are geothermally heated pools in most towns and many villages – see www.swimminginiceland.com for a full list. If you want to do serious lengths, the best pool in Reykjavík is at Laugardalur on Sundlaugavegur (tel: 411 5100; Mon–Fri 6.30am–10pm, Sat–Sun 8am–10pm). It has a 50 metre (160ft) pool, three hot pots, a Jacuzzi, steam room, sun lamps and waterslide.

WHALE-WATCHING

Whale-watching started in Iceland in 1995, but since then the number of companies offering tours has been increasing. There is usually a good chance of seeing something – most likely harbour porpoises and white-beaked dolphins. Of the larger species, the minke whale is most common, although humpbacks, fin and even blue whales are spotted from time to time.

Húsavík, with its excellent Whale Museum, is acknowledged as Iceland's 'whale-watching capital', but there are also departures from Reykjavík, Akureyri, Bíldudalur, Dalvík, Heimaey and Ólafsvík. However, you don't have to be on a boat to see whales – just looking out to sea might reveal a whale's back breaking the surface.

CYCLING

The unmade roads and high winds in much of Iceland can make cycle touring a challenge, to say the least. Off-road cycling is prohibited to help protect the environment.

The **Icelandic Mountain Bike Club** (Íslenski Fjallhjólaklúbburinn, PO Box 5193, 125 Reykjavík, tel: 562 0099, www. fjallahjolaklubburinn.is) is a great source of advice and has suggested itineraries.

GOLF

With 65 courses, golf is thriving in Iceland. Most courses have just nine holes, however there are seventeen 18-hole courses including those in: Reykjavík (Grafarholt and Korpa), Hafnarfjörður (Keilir), Garðabær (Oddur), Hella, Keflavík (Suðurnes), Vestmannaeyjar and Akureyri. For further information contact the **Golf Federation of Iceland** (Golfsamband Íslands, Engjavegur 6, Reykjavík, tel: 514 4050, www.golf.is, http://golficeland.org). The major golfing event in Iceland is the Arctic Open, which takes place in

June each year and is open to professional and amateur golfers alike. The event's host is the **Akureyri Golf Club** (600 Akureyri, tel: 462 2974, www.arcticopen.is).

SHOPPING

Although the 2008 economic crisis was atrocious news for Icelanders, today's weaker króna means that tourists can buy Icelandic goods at cheaper prices, at least compared to those of a few short years ago. It's still not bargain basement – Icelandic products are marketed at those who believe

Golf on the Westman Islands

in paying for quality and smart design. However, the unusual books, music and food on offer, plus beautifully made homeware, clothing and jewellery, will have you reaching for your credit card. In the centre of Reykjavík, most of the tourist shops are in and around Hafnarstræti and Austurstræti, though Laugavegur, leading out of the centre, is home to the majority of the fashion shops. Skólavörðustígur, which branches off Laugavegur at a sharp diagonal, is good for quirky gifts and crafts. In the suburbs are two large malls, Smáralind (www.smaralind.is) and Kringlan (www.kringlan.is), which house most of the usual European high-street chain stores. The biggest, Kringlan, has over 150 shops and food outlets and is easy to reach – it's just a 15-minute bus-ride from the city centre.

For **souvenirs** try Icelandic woollen sweaters, gloves, scarves and hats. Most are produced by small workshops and come in all shapes, sizes and colours. The Handknitting Association of Iceland's shops (Handþrjónasamband Íslands, Skólavörðustigur 19 & Laugavegur 64, http://handknit. is; tel: 552 1890) have a wide selection. Skólavörðustigur has a number of **art** galleries selling some excellent local work, as well as shops selling the best of Icelandic **design**. Duvets, quilts and other bedcovers are also very good quality, although those filled with locally gathered eider down can be expensive.

For traditional **Icelandic music**, try the album Íslensk alþýðulög (Icelandic Folk Songs). There are also fine classical recordings by the Iceland Symphony Orchestra, particularly of works by the late composer Jón Leifs. Of course, Björk and Sigur Rós are Iceland's biggest musical exports, but the

TAX-FREE SHOPPING

On leaving Iceland, you can get a refund of the VAT (Value Added Tax) paid on goods over ISK6,000. The shop assistant will fill out a Tax Free form – keep this safe, along with your purchase receipt. For an immediate refund, take the form to the tax refund points (be prepared to queue) at the Kringlan or Smáralind shopping malls, Reykjavík tourist office, or the counters in the BSÍ bus station, the airport or the Skarfabakki cruise-ship service centre. Otherwise you can get a refund later by post.

If the total is more than ISK5,000 for any one item, you will have to show the goods to customs on your way out of the country, and obtain a customs stamp before you can claim your refund. This does not apply for woollen goods. This scheme can save you up to 15 percent on the price of many items.

modern music scene is ever-changing and new bands appear all the time.

Smoked salmon, roe caviar, dried fish and *skyr*, a delicious Icelandic yoghurt, are good food buys, but be aware of the import restrictions.

NIGHTLIFE

Reykjavík is renowned for its lively weekend nightlife, when jolly drinkers cram into the city's tiny, offbeat and oh-so-cool bars for shouted

Woollen goods on display

conversations, flowing booze, spontaneous musical happenings and dancing.

There are dozens of very welcoming bars and cafés for a drink or light meal during the evening, but the serious clubbing doesn't start until well after midnight – people usually drink at home before going out to party, as bar prices are so high. Icelanders tend to dress up a bit to go out, and there can be long queues outside the most fashionable places on Friday and Saturday. Clubs and pubs open and close in Reykjavík all the time, so it's worth asking around to find out where the newest and most fashionable places are; or check out the free newspaper the *Reykjavík Grapevine* (www.grapevine.is), which takes its gigs and nightlife seriously.

Reykjavík also has a thriving **cultural** scene – *What's On in Reykjavík* and local papers list the latest music, dance and theatre performances. The city's dazzling harbour concert hall, Harpa, is home to both the Icelandic Opera

and the internationally acclaimed Iceland Symphony Orchestra, which perform there from September to mid-June. Outside those months, there is a packed summer programme of pop, rock and classical music events, both in and outside of Reykjavík – see www.icelandmusic.is for details.

Reykjavík has a good selection of stylish bars

ACTIVITIES FOR CHILDREN

Icelanders try to involve children in almost all their sporting and cultural activities. Swimming and horse riding are particularly popular with local children, and families gather in large numbers at weekends to feed the ducks and geese at Tjörnin in front of City Hall.

The pool at Laugardalur (see page 97) has a huge 85m (280ft) waterslide and a children's pool. At the same site, Reykjavík's Zoo and Family Park (www.mu.is; daily 10am–6pm, until 5pm in winter, free for under-fives) is always a hit with small kids, and when they tire of looking at the seals, foxes, reindeer, horses, cows and pigs, they can head for the Family Park and climb a replica Viking ship and cross a man-made lake on a raft. There is a large grill that can be used free of charge for barbecuing. The seals are fed twice a day (11am and 4pm).

For older children there are two bowling rinks (keiluhöllin, tel: 511 5300; http://keiluhollin.is; Sun–Thu 2–10.30pm, until 1pm on Fri, Sat 11am–1am,) at Öskjuhlíð near Perlan, and in the Egilshöll sports facility in the suburb of Grafarvogur.

CALENDAR OF EVENTS

Precise dates change from year to year. Check with tourist offices.

6 January Twelfth Night, marked with songs, bonfires and fireworks.

February Þorrablót. The half-way point of winter, this festival involves eating delicacies including lambs' heads and testicles, and cured shark.

Early February Festival of Lights. Reykjavík's winter festival with arts and cultural events..

Early March. Food & Fun Festival. A week-long culinary feast, attracting the best chiefs from the US and Europe who then team up with local restaurants to create original yet affordable menus; www.foodandfun.is.

1st Thursday after April 18th The First Day of Summer. Marked by parades, sports events and the giving of summer-themed gifts.

1st Sunday in June Festival of the Sea. Celebrations in all coastal communities with sports and dances.

17 June National Day. Formal ceremonies in the morning and partying and fairs all afternoon and evening.

May/June Reykjavík Arts Festival (http://en.listahatid.is). A two-week celebration of music, theatre, art and dance.

Early July (biannual) Landsmót National Horse Show (www.landsmot.is), held in different towns.

1st Monday in August Summer Bank Holiday. A long weekend for all Icelanders, with open-air pop festivals around the country.

August. Reykjavík Jazz Festival. An annual jazz feast with international stars; http://reykjavikjazz.is/.

September/October Reykjavík Film Festival (www.riff.is). A 10-day extravaganza featuring both Icelandic and international movies.

Late October Iceland Airwaves (www.icelandairwaves.is). A five-day tidal-wave of international indie/pop/rock.

23 December St Þorláksmessa. Feast-day of Iceland's patron saint; the high point of the pre-Christmas celebrations.

31 December New Year's Eve. A satirical revue on television, followed by night-long outdoor parties with bonfires and fireworks.

EATING OUT

Dining out in Iceland has undergone tremendous changes in the past 20 years. Many Icelandic chefs have sought training abroad, then returned home to apply their new-found gourmet knowledge to traditional ingredients. The restaurant scene has been hit by a great wave of energy, enthusiasm and experimentation, and dining out in Reykjavík is consequently a real treat. Prices are not low in Iceland's better restaurants – but you are paying for excellent meals made with high-quality ingredients.

Iceland was effectively cut off from the rest of Europe for centuries, and, with very little in the way of food imports, no Icelandic *haute cuisine* developed. The population depended on what they could catch or grow themselves, making do with a diet based almost entirely on fish, lamb and vegetables such as potatoes. Various methods were devised to preserve the food so it could be used for months after it was caught. Meat was smoked, salted and pickled. Fish would be hung out and dried, or smoked in dung or salted, or even buried. You

MEAL TIMES

Icelanders tend to have their main meal in the middle of the day and this is also when you can find some of the better priced all-inclusive menus (often restricted to around noon–2.30pm). In Reykjavík and many of the larger towns, restaurants tend to be open all day from about 11.30am until 11pm (later at weekends), so you don't have to be too organised about when you eat. In some smaller places, cafés and restaurants shut at about 2.30pm and reopen around 7pm. They close any time after 10pm, so it's always a good idea to check their opening times before planning your evening. Breakfast hours are relaxed, so you don't usually have to be up too early to fit in with them.

Fresh fish is a staple in Iceland

will still occasionally see fish-drying racks on the hillsides as you drive around the country.

TRADITIONAL FOODS

The two staple foods are fish and lamb. Fish is most plentiful and cheaper, so every meal, from breakfast onwards, will usually include it in some form. Wind-dried cod or haddock, *harðfiskur*, is a popular snack. It is torn into strips, tenderised and eaten with butter, accompanied with a glass of milk or maybe something stronger.

Whalemeat *(hval)*, mostly from minke whales, is rarely eaten by Icelanders anymore, but it is commonly found on menus in tourist restaurants. The International Fund for Animal Welfare (IFAW), concerned that the Icelandic whaling industry is largely sustained by tourist consumption, has launched the 'Meet Us, Don't Eat Us' campaign to draw visitors' attention to the problem. Whalemeat is usually soaked first in milk to extract some of the oil, and then served as medallions or steaks.

One of Iceland's most notorious food rituals is the ceremonious intake of rotten shark (*hákarl*) and schnapps. After being buried for three months or more, shark becomes acrid and ammoniac; rubbery and rotten, it is washed down in small cubes with ample quantities of the Icelandic spirit, *brennivín*.

Most Icelandic seafood, by contrast, is absolutely delicious and comes to your plate very fresh indeed. Icelandic cod, halibut, turbot and monkfish, for example, are juicy and succulent. Salmon and trout from the rivers are large and relatively inexpensive, as is char, a species of trout that is found all over Iceland. Smoked salmon and gravadlax (smoked salmon marinated with herbs) are both of very high quality.

While you will never go short of tasty fish, you might tire of it after a while. The other Icelandic staple, lamb, may cost more, but the taste is exceptional. Sheep farms on the island are small, and the flocks are allowed to graze wild in the

Café Riis in Holmavík serves up delicious meals

highlands, where they eat herbs as well as grass. As a result, the meat has quite a gamey flavour.

As with fish, lamb was traditionally smoked to produce *hangikjöt*, which is eaten hot or cold. Nothing was ever allowed to go to waste in winter in Iceland, and dishes made of sheep's offal are still produced. *Slátur* (literally 'slaughter') is a haggis-like dish made from all manner of left-overs, pressed into cakes, pickled in whey and cooked in stomach lining. Alternatively *svið* are boiled and singed sheep's heads, minus the brains, that are eaten either fresh or pickled. The meat is sometimes then taken off the bone and pressed to produce *sviðasulta*. A real delicacy, served on special occasions, is *súrsaðir hrútspungar* (pickled rams' testicles).

A limited amount of game finds its way onto the dinner plate. Reindeer from the east of the country is similar to venison. Ptarmigan is a grouse-like bird and a favourite at Christmas time. Icelanders are quite happy to eat those cute little puffins too; the bird is frequently smoked and produces quite a dark, rich meat.

The main locally produced vegetables are potatoes and turnips. Wild berries are often used in sauces and puddings, and rhubarb thrives in the cold climate. Otherwise, the dessert course is often cakes or pastries. One delicious treat is *skyr*, a yoghurt-type dish made of pasteurised skimmed milk and live bacteria; it's often mixed with fruit flavouring and is high in calcium and low in calories.

Bread, often made with rye, is a normal accompaniment to any meal. It may be baked in underground ovens in the naturally hot earth to produce *hverabrauð* ('steam bread'). Rye

Beer ban

Drinking beer was illegal in Iceland from 1915–89. Its reintroduction – on 1 March 1989 – is celebrated annually as *Bjórdagurinn* (Beer Day).

pancakes, known as *flatkaka*, go well with smoked salmon and other smorgasbord-type toppings.

WHAT TO DRINK

Not surprisingly, the Icelandic climate is not conducive to wine-growing, so all wines are imported and therefore extremely expensive.

Traditionally, drinking alcohol mid-week has not been part of Icelandic culture, although it is becoming more common to have a glass of wine or beer with a meal when dining out. A strong Protestant work ethic is usually cited as the cause... along with the inflated price of alcohol. The bottle that is expensive enough at the state liquor store (*vínbúðar*) will invariably be around three times more expensive at a restaurant. Even house wines generally cost around ISK800–1,100 per glass, and a decent bottle of wine in a good restaurant will cost upwards of ISK5,000. Beer, while not exactly inexpensive, is generally a more affordable ISK1000 per half litre.

Icelandic spirits, on the other hand, are both strong and tasty. *Brennivín* ('burnt wine') is a schnapps distilled from potatoes and flavoured with caraway seeds. Its nickname is 'Black Death', which gives an idea of its strength. A good variant is *Hvannarótar*, which is flavoured with angelica.

Coffee is the national drink of Iceland, consumed from early morning to late at night, at home, at work or even walking down the street. Refills are usually included if you buy a cup of standard coffee in a café, and some petrol stations have a free jug on the counter for their petrol-buying customers. Classic rocket-fuel is supplemented countrywide by espressos, cappuccinos, macchiatos and lattes.

MENU READER
Gætum við/get ég fengið... Could we/I have...

BASICS
ávextir fruit
bakað baked
baunir peas, beans
brauð bread
grilluð grilled
grænmeti vegetables
hrísgrjón rice
kartöflur potatoes
laukur onion
ostar cheeses
reykt smoked
salat salad
smjör butter
smárettir snacks
soðið boiled
steikt fried
súpa soup

DRINKS
appelsínusafi orange juice
bjór beer
kaffi coffee
mjólk milk
te tea
vatn water
vín wine
(hrauðvín) (red)
(hvítvín) (white)

FISKUR (FISH)
bleikja char
hörpuskel scallop
humar lobster
lax salmon
lúða halibut
rauðspretta plaice
sandhverfa turbot
síld herring
silungur trout
skötuselur monkfish
steinbítur catfish
ýsa haddock
rækja shrimp
þorskur cod

KJÖT (MEAT)
Kjúklingur chicken
Lambakjöt lamb
Lambakótelettur lamb chop
lundi puffin
nautakjöt beef
nautalundir beef fillet
nautasteik beef steak
skinka ham
svínakjöt pork
lítið steikt rare
miðlungs steikt medium
vel steikt well done

PLACES TO EAT

We have used the following symbols to give an idea of the price for a three-course meal for one, excluding wine:

$$$$** over ISK10,000   **$$ ISK2,500–5,000
$$$** ISK5,000–10,000   **$ below ISK2,500

REYKJAVÍK

Austur India Fjélagið $$$ *Hverfisgata 56, tel: 552 1630,* http://
austurindia.is. Indian spices and Icelandic ingredients turn out to
be a perfect match: celebrate the happy marriage at this great lit-
tle restaurant. The menu favours cuisine from the northwest of
India in the form of its succulent tandoori dishes, along with tur-
meric, tamarind and ginger-flavoured delights from other regions.

Dill $$$ *Nordic House, Hverfisgötu 12, tel: 552 1522,* http://dill
restaurant.is. A gourmet's delight, this elegant Scandinavian
restaurant specialises in local, organic ingredients cooked in
contemporary 'Nordic Kitchen' style. Prepare yourself for mouth-
watering dishes such as smoked haddock with blue mussels,
reindeer with blueberry sauce, and almond cake with cinnamon
ice-cream. Open Wed–Sat from 6pm.

The Gallery Restaurant $$$$ *Bergstaðastræti 37, tel: 552 5700,*
www.holt.is. The Gallery Restaurant (inside Hotel Holt) is arguably
the best restaurant in the capital, with a magnificent display of
Icelandic art. The award-winning chef uses fresh local produce,
including a wide range of fish, reindeer and lamb, and presents
the dishes with creativity. It is particularly renowned for its lobster
soup, the recipe perfected over 50 years. Closed Sun–Mon.

Gló $$ *Laugavegur 20b, tel: 553 1111,* www.glo.is. Vitamin-de-
prived diners should head for canteen-style Gló, whose healthy
menus soon put colour back into your cheeks. Four tasty dishes
of the day (one raw-food; one chicken; one vegetarian; and one
soup) are on offer, with at least half the ingredients guaranteed
organic. And if all this virtue gets too much, there's also a tempt-
ing cake board...

Icelandic Fish & Chips $$ *Tryggvagata 11, tel: 511 1118,* www.fish andchips.is. The fish and chips here are given a healthy spin, made with organic potatoes and the freshest quality fish. No wheat or sugar is used in the fish batter, the chips are roasted rather than deep-fried, and the unusual selection of dressings is made using low-fat, yoghurt-like *skyr*. It does a roaring trade in takeaways, too.

Jómfrúin $ *Lækjargata 4, tel: 551 0100,* www.jomfruin.is. An excellent choice for lunch, when the restaurant is full of homesick Danes. A seemingly endless choice of filling Danish-style open sandwiches. Choose carefully and lunch need not cost more than ISK2,500.

Kaffivagninn $$ *Grandagarði 10, tel: 551 5932,* http://kaffivagninn. is. Open since 1935, this is arguably the oldest restaurant in Reykjavik. Located near the harbour, it boasts fantastic views. The menu is short, but has an excellent choice of Scandinavian and Icelandic meals. Good place for breakfast or Sunday brunch. Opens daily only until 6pm.

Kol Restaurant $$–$$$ *Skólavörðustígur 40, tel: 517 7474,* http:// kolrestaurant.is. This small, cosy venue offers a great selection of fish and meat dishes that are prepared using local ingredients. The dinner tasting and gourmet menus are excellent, but expensive; the set lunch menu won't exceed ISK4,000. There are also vegetarian options. Open every day for dinner and Mon–Fri for lunch.

Lækjarbrekka $$$ *Bankastræti 2, tel: 551 4430,* www.laekjar brekka.is. In an atmospheric timber building dating from 1834, this cosy restaurant with period furniture, chandeliers and heavy drapes is known for its gourmet set menus featuring lobster, puffin or lamb. It is an excellent choice for a special occasion. Finish off with a drink in the snug lounge upstairs.

Ostabúðin $$$ *Skólavörðustíg 8, tel: 562 2772,* http://ostabudin.is. Undoubtedly one of the city's best and most popular restaurants. You can't book an evening table, so it can be difficult to avoid the queue. A short, but well-thought and executed menu never fails to tantalise the taste buds. The fish soup is a must. Good value for money.

Café Paris $$ *Austurstræti 14, tel: 551 1020*, www.cafeparis.is. A Reykjavík classic, this cosy little cafe overlooking Austurvöllur square and the Parliament Buildings, has been here as long as anyone can remember. Quintessentially Parisian in style and feel, this is a good choice for a light lunch and a good cup of coffee. In summer there is outdoor seating.

Skólabrú $$$ *Pósthússtræti 17, tel: 511 1690*, www.skolabru.is. A stylishly chic restaurant mixing old-world charm with Nordic minimalism. Top-notch service and beautifully presented food. The menu has both Icelandic and international dishes, with an emphasis on seafood, duck and game.

Restaurant Silfur $$$$ *Pósthússtræti 11, tel: 551 1440*, www.hotel borg.is. Situated on the ground floor of Hotel Borg, this is certainly an elegant place surrounded by Art Deco splendour. Imagine that you are back in the 1930s – except, of course, for the distinctly modern prices. The menu is eclectic and includes delights such as smoked puffin breast in a beetroot sauce.

Vegamót $$ *Vegamótastígur 4, tel: 511 3040*, www.vegamot.is. An extremely popular bistro in the centre of town serving a varied menu of good-value food: everything from fresh fish to TexMex dishes. Plentiful brunch options are available until 4pm on Saturday and Sunday. It is also a relatively cheap place for a beer.

Þrir Frakkar $$ *Baldursgata 14, tel: 552 3939*, www.3frakkar.com. This cosy neighbourhood French-style bistro serves up an accomplished menu of authentic Icelandic dishes, including the traditional plokkfiskur, a kind of fish and potato mash.

SOUTH AND SOUTHEAST

Kaffi Krús $$ *Austurvegur 7, Selfoss, tel: 482 1266*, www.kaffi krus.is. Selfoss is hardly the loveliest Icelandic town, but it's the nearest large settlement to the Golden Circle. Break up your sightseeing with lunch at this warm, welcoming bistro, set in a creaky-floored old wooden house. The menu offers all manner of burgers, sandwiches, pasta dishes, served up in relaxed surroundings.

Lava Restaurant $$$$ *Blue Lagoon, Grindavík, tel: 420 8800*, www.bluelagoon.com. Eat overlooking the thermal spa at this world-famous spot. The menu uses fish brought ashore at the nearby harbour in a variety of international dishes including bouillabaisse and curried cod, cooked up by Iceland's Chef of the Year 2013. Best enjoyed after, rather than before, a dip in the hot waters.

Við Fjöruborðið $$$ *Eyrarbraut 3a, Stokkseyri, tel: 483 1550*, www. fjorubordid.is. Reykjavík residents drive the 70km (40 miles) to Stokkseyri simply to dine at Við Fjöruborðið. This atmospheric seaside restaurant specialises in lobster, and is said to have the best lobster soup in Iceland.

EAST AND NORTHEAST

Bautinn $$ *Hafnarstræti 92, Akureyri, tel: 462 1818*, www.bautinn. is. A good choice in the centre of Akureyri for burgers, pizzas, no-nonsense fry-ups and simple meat and fish dishes.

Gamli Bærinn $$ *Beside Hotel Reynihlíð, Mývatn, tel: 464 4270*,www. myvatnhotel.is/en/home-gamli. The name means 'old farm', and the building, which dates from 1912, is by the architect who designed Reykjavík's Parliament. The place is now a delightful little restaurant and café, where fantastic char soup is served. With live jazz and local bands at the weekend.

Rub 23 $$$ *Kaupvangsstræti 6, Akureyri, tel: 462 2223*, www.rub23. is/en. If you like to play with your food, this polished fish restaurant is the place for you. First choose your trout (or lamb, chicken or beef), pick one of the 11 'rubs' as a marinade, then wait for the chef to cook your special combination – it's a little like watching a row of cherries come up on a fruit machine. There's also a sushi selection, and a recommended tasting menu.

Strikið $$$ *Skipagata 14, Akureyri, tel: 462 7100,* www.strikid.is. It looks like an unpromising office block from the outside, but this is a good-quality restaurant in the heart of Akureyri with unsurpassed views of the fjord and mountains from its fifth-floor location. The restaurant serves burgers, pizzas, meat and fish dishes.

WEST AND NORTHWEST

Búðarklettur $$ *Brákarbraut 13-15, Borgarnes, tel: 437 1600,* www. landnam.is. The Settlement Centre's restaurant serves hearty pasta, fish and meat mains. Many have a traditional slant – think smoked lamb and herring on rye bread – and there's a larger vegetarian selection than in most Icelandic restaurants.

Hótel Buðir Restaurant $$$$ *Main Road, Buðir, 356 Snæfellsbær; tel: 435 6700,* www.hotelbudir.is. Reopened after a devastating fire, this is one of Iceland's finest hotels. Seafood and game predominate in its oceanfront restaurant, including honey-glazed catfish with ginger, chilli and liquorice sauce.

Hótel Flókalundur $$$ *Vatnsfjörður, 451 Patreksfjörður; tel: 456 2011,* www.flokalundur.is/dining. This is the only restaurant in the vicinity. Rosemary-roasted trout with butter-fried vegetables, roast lamb and garlic lobster are some of the evening meals served. Also a popular coffee stop for people waiting for the ferry to Snæfellsnes. Open 10 May to 20 September.

Núpur Guesthouse $$$ *Dýrafjörður, Þingeyri district, tel: 456 8235.* A small, but select evening menu is served (7–9pm) in summer. Fish takes pride of place, along with the restaurant's speciality, goat meat.

Café Riis $$ *Hafnarbraut 39, Holmavík, tel: 451 3567,*www.caferiis. is. A tasteful café/bar/restaurant with pizzas, burgers, freshly caught fish, and Icelandic dishes such as puffin breast with blueberries or smoked lumpfish.

Við Pollinn $$$ *Hótel Ísafjörður, Silfurtorgi 2, Ísafjörður, tel: 456 3360,* www.vidpollinn.is. The most upmarket place in town to eat, with excellent fish dishes and superb views of the fjord.

A-Z TRAVEL TIPS

A Summary of Practical Information

A Accommodation 116
  Airports 116
B Bicycle Rental 117
  Budgeting for
     Your Trip 117
C Camping 119
  Car Hire 119
  Climate 120
  Clothing 121
  Crime and Safety ...121
D Driving........... 121
E Electricity 123
  Embassies and
     Consulates 123
  Emergencies.......123
G Gay and Lesbian
     Travellers....... 124
  Getting There 124
  Guides and Tours ...125
H Health and Medical
     Care 125

L Language 126
M Maps 127
  Media........... 127
  Money 128
O Opening Times 129
P Police........... 129
  Post Offices....... 129
  Public Holidays.... 130
T Telephones 131
  Time Zones 131
  Tipping.......... 131
  Toilets 131
  Tourist
     Information 132
  Transport......... 132
V Visas and Entry
     Requirements ... 133
W Websites and
     Internet Access.. 134
Y Youth Hostels 134

ACCOMMODATION (See also Camping, Youth Hostels, and the list of Recommended Hotels, see page 135)

The Icelandic Tourist Board (www.visiticeland.com) operates a (voluntary) classification system for accommodation, which grades hotels from five stars, for those with the best facilities, down to one star, for the most basic.

Both in Reykjavík and elsewhere in the country, many of the higher-rated hotels are large and impersonal. The capital has some quality hotels with character, and there are one or two elsewhere in the country, but these are the exception. Overall, Icelandic hotels can be quite spartan; and all Icelandic buildings have thin walls and curtains – light sleepers should bring earplugs and an eye mask. In summer, 11 of Iceland's schools, universities and conference centres open as 'summer hotels' (www.hoteledda.is). If you are doing a lot of walking or horse riding check if the hotel has a sauna, hot-tub or pool, all of which will be geothermally heated.

There are guesthouses everywhere in Iceland and these are generally welcoming and considerably cheaper than hotels. They vary in quality, but are invariably clean and well-kept. Bathrooms are very often shared. Farmhouse accommodation is also available. More than 170 farms operate through Icelandic Farm Holidays (tel: 570 2700, www.farmholidays.is).

If you are travelling around, the location of a hotel will probably be more important to you than its facilities. Local tourist offices (see page 132) have comprehensive lists of nearby hotels and staff who can speak English and make reservations for you. If you are travelling between May and September you are advised to book ahead.

AIRPORTS

99.9 percent of international flights arrive at **Keflavík International Airport** (tel: 425 6000, www.kefairport.is), 50km (31 miles) from Reykjavík. After every flight arrival, the Flybus (www.re.is/flybus) transfer coach transports passengers to the BSÍ bus terminal about 1.5km (1 mile) from the centre of Reykjavík. The journey takes about 45 minutes and costs from ISK1,950: buy tickets from the ticket machine or ticket booth next to the airport exit. The Airport Express (https://airportex-press.is) runs between the airport and more than 160 drop off points (door-to-door service), including the Reykjavik bus terminal. Taxis from the airport to central Reykjavík will take 30–45 minutes and will cost approximately ISK17,000.

From mid-May to September, some charter flights use Akureyri airport, located around 3km (1.86 miles) south of town. There are also seasonal flights to Greenland from Akureyri.

Reykjavík's Domestic Airport (tel: 570 3000) is at the other end of the runway from the Icelandair Hotel Reykjavík Natura, and there are regular buses to and from the city centre. **Air Iceland** (tel: 570 3030; www.airiceland.is) offers scheduled services to most parts of the country.

B

BICYCLE RENTAL

Some places around Iceland hire out bikes; make enquiries at tourist offices, hotels and campsites. Cycling is popular around Lake Mývatn: Hotel Reynihlíð and the Hlíð and Bjarg campsites have a reasonable selection. **Reykjavík Bike Tours** (101 Reykjavík, tel: 694 8956, http://icelandbike.com) have rentals and tours.

BUDGETING FOR YOUR TRIP

Following the 2008 financial crisis, Iceland went from being eye-wateringly expensive to merely expensive for foreign visitors.

Getting to Iceland. The main airline serving Iceland is Icelandair, operating from both Europe and North America. Budget airlines WOW Air (wowair.co.uk/) and easyJet (www.easyjet.com) have slightly cheaper flights from various European cities. In summer it is essential to book well in advance to secure the lowest fares. In the UK, Icelandair have fares from London Gatwick, London Heathrow, Manchester and Glasgow from £344 return. For a cheaper option, try WOW, where rates start from about £100. Investigate special packages and offers on www.icelandair.co.uk. If you are flying from the US you can expect to pay from $900 for a return ticket.

Accommodation. Top summer prices in Reykjavík are over ISK30,000 for a twin room in a luxury hotel, with en-suite shower or bath, and breakfast included. Guesthouses charge from ISK20,000. Out of season, prices can drop by around 40 percent. In some places you pay about half the price if you use your own sleeping-bag.

Meals. A sit-down lunch in a restaurant costs from ISK1,500 (but look out for cheap lunchtime buffet deals), and dinner from ISK2,500. Alcohol is expensive, with a glass of beer in a restaurant costing around ISK800 and a bottle of wine upwards of ISK5,000. It's a good idea to bring your maximum duty-free allowance with you from home.

Local transport. Reykjavík's city bus service is good value, with bus tickets costing ISK420. Taxis are costly – the meter starts running as soon as the vehicle pulls up to your hotel, and a trip from Reykjavík to the international airport costs around ISK17,000 (compared to the Flybus ticket price of ISK2,200). There are various long-distance bus passes available for summer journeys from Iceland on your Own (tel: 580 5400, www.icelandonyourown.is).

Generally, if you visit during the summer, stay in decent hotels, eat out in restaurants most nights and undertake a few activities, you should expect to pay upwards of ISK30,000 per person per day, based on two people sharing. However, it is possible to cut costs by staying in guesthouses or youth hostels and eating the odd meal in a restaurant – for this, you should reckon on about ISK20,000 per day. Camping and self-catering will cost around ISK10,000 per day.

Domestic flights can be cheaper than buses: so-called 'net offers' are available on most Air Iceland flights, which when booked in advance help to secure the best price for any particular flight. For example, a single bus ticket from the capital to Akureyri costs about ISK9,000, while the lowest 'net offer' air fare costs about ISK8,000.

Incidentals. A three-hour sightseeing tour of Reykjavík costs about ISK6,000 per person, and a Golden Circle day tour to Gullfoss, Geysir and Þingvellir is ISK10,000. Whale-watching costs from ISK9,000. On-the-spot car hire costs around ISK18,000 per day (around half the price if you book online before you travel; price for medium size car). A spa treatment such as a 30-minute massage will cost from ISK12,000. A coffee costs from ISK400, a cinema ticket costs ISK1,500, and an Icelandic knitted jumper will cost from ISK8,500.

C

CAMPING

There are around 70 registered campsites in Iceland, although you can camp almost anywhere if you get the landowners' permission. Within national parks and conservation areas, camping is only allowed at designated spots. Official campsites are found in most towns and villages, at national parks, conservation areas, places of natural beauty and some farms and community centres. The standard varies. Expect to pay from ISK1400 per person per night for anything from a layer of pumice and an earth closet, to soft turf and hot showers. The recognised sites are open from mid-May or June to August or mid-September.

The Iceland Tourist Board (www.visiticeland.com) has camping listings on its website. Easy equipment hire is available in Reykjavík from companies such as Iceland Camping Equipment, (www.iceland-camping-equipment.com, Klapparstígur 16).

CAR HIRE (See also Driving and Budgeting for your Trip)

Several major international rental companies are represented in Iceland, as well as locally based firms. Prices are high. You must be at least 21 years old to hire a car in Iceland. Insurance is compulsory and not always included in the quoted price, so check first.

The following companies offer a full range of vehicles: Hertz (tel: 522 4400, www.hertz.is), Europcar (tel: 461 6000, 568 6915, www.europcar.is), Avis (tel: 591 4000, www.avis.is), SADCARS (tel: 577 6300, http://sadcars.com). Many hire companies offer one-way rentals, allowing you to drive from Reykjavík to Akureyri, for example, and then return by air.

It is worthwhile going over your intended route with the rental company to check what roads are allowed for your type of vehicle. Note that insurance companies will not cover hire cars taken into the interior or on F-roads.

CLIMATE

Influenced by the warm Gulf Stream and prevailing southwesterly winds, Iceland's temperate oceanic climate is surprisingly mild for the latitude. However, summers are generally cool, and the country is often wet and windy, with the weather changing dramatically from day to day, or even hourly. Basically, it's sensible to be prepared for all eventualities. The weather is drier and sunnier in the north and east than the south and west, although no less windy. The south coast is notoriously wet.

You can get weather information in English by calling tel: 902 0600 or visiting www.vedur.is/english.

Average rainfall and temperatures:

	J	F	M	A	M	J	J	A	S	O	N	D
°C min	-2	-2	1	1	4	7	9	8	6	3	0	-2
°C max	2	3	4	6	10	12	14	14	11	7	4	2
Rainfall (mm)	76	72	82	58	44	50	52	62	66	85	72	79

CLOTHING

In summer, light woollens or a fleece, and a wind- and rainproof jacket or coat are essential, along with something for warmer days (wearing layers works best in Iceland's changeable summer weather). Take plenty of jumpers to keep you warm plus thick walking socks (and thinner ones to go against your skin).

Icelanders are very clothes-conscious, which is reflected in Reykjavík's fashion shops. If you plan to eat out at one of the city's better restaurants, you should dress up. Although most pubs are casual, people do get dressed up to go to smarter bars, and a few clubs maintain a policy of no jeans or trainers.

Pack a swimming costume, as geothermal bathing pools are very much a part of the Icelandic social scene.

CRIME AND SAFETY (See also Emergencies and Police)

Iceland is an extremely peaceful and law-abiding nation. Of the few people in prison, most are drugs offenders. Public places are well lit. Violent crime is virtually non-existent, bar the odd domestic dispute and drunken brawl. The latter is most likely on Friday and Saturday nights, when the city's youth takes to the streets of central Reykjavík on a (mostly good-humoured) drunken spree.

D

DRIVING

Despite the high cost of car hire, rental may provide the only way to see everything you wish in the time available. Driving in Iceland can also be a real pleasure – the roads are not busy and the freedom to stop to admire the scenery or go for a walk is a huge bonus. Be prepared for journeys to take a lot longer than you might expect from the distances involved.

Road conditions. While much of the main highway encircling the country is surfaced, many routes in Iceland are just gravel or unmade and full of potholes. Some roads are prone to flooding, and bridges are often single-lane. Livestock make frequent mad dashes into the middle of the road.

Sandstorms can be a hazard along the coast and in some parts of the interior. In winter, snow and ice are common, and studded snow tyres are essential. For information on road conditions call tel: 1778 or check on www.vegagerdin.is.

Rules and regulations. Icelanders drive on the right. The speed limit is 50kmh (30mph) in urban areas, 80kmh (50mph) on gravel roads in rural areas and 90kmh (55mph) on asphalt roads out of the towns.

Driving off roads is illegal (fines are extremely high), seat belts are compulsory in the front and back of a car, and headlights must be used at all times, day and night. Drink-driving is taken very seriously by the authorities – it is against the law to drive a vehicle in Iceland after consuming any alcohol. Offenders lose their licences and face heavy fines. Mobile phones must be used with a hands-free set while driving.

Fuel. In Reykjavík there are several 24-hour filling stations. Those that close overnight usually have automatic pumps that take banknotes or credit cards (but check that yours works while the kiosk is still manned!). Around the ring road there are filling stations every 50km (30 miles) or so, but if in doubt fill up before you move on. Petrol costs approximately ISK200 per litre.

Parking. Reykjavík has plenty of parking meters, ticket machines and car parks, some of which are covered and attended. On-street parking can be hard to find. Elsewhere in the country you will encounter few problems, and there are large free car parks at most of the major tourist sites.

Einbreið brú Single-lane bridge (often marked by flashing orange lights)
Malbik endar Unmade road
Blindhæð Blind summit

Road signs. The usual international symbols are used on road signs, but look out also for:

Help and information. Tourist boards have leaflets about driving on unmade roads and in winter, as well as lists of all road signs. Also see the website www.safetravel.is.

E

ELECTRICITY

The electric current in Iceland is 220 volts, 50 Hz AC. Plugs are European round pin with two prongs.

EMBASSIES AND CONSULATES

Australia: Australian Embassy in Copenhagen, Denmark, tel: (+45) 70 26 36 76, www.denmark.embassy.gov.au

Canada: Túngata 14, 101 Reykjavík, tel: 575 6500, www.canada.is

Ireland: Honorary Consul in Reykjavík, Mr David Thorsteinsson, tel: 554 2355, e-mail: davidcsh@islandia.is

South Africa: Consul General Mr Jón R. Magnússon, Þorragata 5, Reykjavík, tel: 561 7181, email: jr@mi.is

United Kingdom: Laufásvegur 31, 101 Reykjavík, tel: 550 5100, www.gov.uk/government/world/organisations/british-embassy-reykjavik

United States: Laufásvegur 21, 101 Reykjavík, tel: 595 2200, http://iceland.usembassy.gov

The Icelandic Foreign Ministry has a full list of diplomatic representatives on its website: www.mfa.is

EMERGENCIES (See also Health and Medical Care)

To contact the police, ambulance, fire service or other emergency situations, tel: **112**.

In case of serious illness or accidents, there is a 24-hour casualty department in Landspítali University Hospital (Fossvogur, tel: 543 2000).

Chemists are signed *Apótek*, and there is at least one in every town. Lyfja (Lágmúli 5, Reykjavík, tel: 533 2300) is open daily from 8am–midnight.

In case of dental emergencies, tel: 575 0505.

G

GAY AND LESBIAN TRAVELLERS

Iceland has a tolerant attitude towards gays and lesbians. The country had the world's first openly gay prime minister, and passed a gender-neutral marriage bill in 2010.

For information and advice contact: The Gay and Lesbian Association/Samtökin '78, 4th Floor, Suðurgata 3, 101 Reykjavík, tel: 552 7878, e-mail: office@samtokin78.is, www.samtokin78.is. Open Mon–Fri 1–4pm; on Thursday evenings there is a library and a coffee bar, open 8–11pm.

There is an annual Gay Pride celebration in Reykjavík every August, www.facebook.com/reykjavikpride/. More information about the gay scene in Iceland can be found at www.gayice.is.

GETTING THERE (See also Airports and Budgeting)

The fastest and cheapest way to get to Iceland is by air. **Icelandair** (www.icelandair.co.uk/www.icelandair.com) is the main airline serving Iceland, operating from both Europe and North America. In the UK, Icelandair serves London Gatwick, London Heathrow, Manchester and Glasgow. In North America; Boston, Chicago, Denver, Edmonton, Houston, Halifax, Minneapolis, New York, Orlando, Portland, Seattle, Toronto, Vancouver (seasonal) and Washington, among others.

Budget airline **WOW Air** (wowair.co.uk) has daily year-round departures from London Gatwick, Bristol and Edinburgh. The airline also flies year-round to Boston, Los Angeles, New York, Toronto, Montreal, San Francisco and Washington.

easyJet (www.easyjet.com) has year-round departures from London Luton, Bristol, Edinburgh and Manchester.

The Faroese company, **Smyril Line** www.smyrilline.com, operates a weekly (twice a week in summer) ferry service to Iceland. The ship Norröna sails from Hirtshals in Denmark to Seyðisfjörður in eastern Iceland, calling in at Tórshavn (Faroe Islands).

GUIDES AND TOURS (See also Public Transport)

One of the best ways of seeing the main sites is by organised coach tours. The drivers and tour leaders are always well informed and speak English. If you want to travel into the interior or onto glaciers, a tour is often the only choice.

Tours are well run, and many allow you to do some exploring by yourself. **Reykjavík Excursions** (BSI Bus Terminal, 101 Reykjavík, tel: 580 5400, www.re.is) are the biggest providers of day tours from Reykjavík to the west and southwest of the country, including whale-watching, the Blue Lagoon and glacier tours.

Tours can last from half a day to three weeks. As well as sightseeing there are tours specialising in hiking, geology, birdwatching, fishing and horse riding. Sports-orientated tours have good-quality equipment and guides who are fully trained for the environment. For full details, contact the Icelandic Tourist Office (www.visiticeland.com).

H

HEALTH AND MEDICAL CARE (See also Emergencies)

Thanks to its clean air and low pollution, Iceland is an extremely healthy place. The water is clean to drink, although you should never drink from glacial rivers or streams. No vaccinations are required to visit Iceland. The standard of medical care is very high, but nonetheless, all visitors should have adequate medical insurance, though an agreement exists between Iceland, the UK and

Scandinavian countries for limited health insurance coverage of its residents. Travellers from those countries should obtain the European Health Insurance Card (EHIC) before leaving home.

Despite the high latitude, the Icelandic sun can still burn, especially when reflected off snow and ice. Sunblock and good sunglasses should be worn if you are outside for long periods.

In extreme circumstances hypothermia is a possibility. Symptoms include shivering, numbness, dizzy spells and confused behaviour. If affected, take shelter, remove and replace wet clothing, and consume hot drinks and high-calorie food.

Every year all too many visitors are injured, sometimes very seriously, by putting feet or hands into boiling hot mud pools and springs, so take care to avoid this. If you are planning to take part in any unusual or 'dangerous' sports, make sure that these are covered by your policy.

L

LANGUAGE

Icelandic is a Germanic language and has barely changed since Viking times. Although it is grammatically complex, anyone who speaks one of the other Scandinavian languages or German will recognise words and features. Thankfully, though, there is no need to master Icelandic to enjoy a holiday in Iceland, since nearly all Icelanders speak excellent English, particularly the young.

yes **já**
no **nei**
hello/hi **halló/hæ**
good morning/afternoon **góðan dáginn**
good evening **gott kvöld**
good night **góða nótt**

goodbye **bless**
How do you do? Sæll (to a man); sæl (to a woman)
Fine, thanks. **Mél líður vel, takk.**
thank you **takk fyrir**
yesterday/today/tomorrow **í gær/í dag/á morgun**
Where/when/how? **Hvar/hvenær/hvernig?**
How long/how far? **Hvað lengi/hversu langt?**
left/right **vinstri/hægri**
hot/cold **heitt/kalt**
old/new **gamalt/ungt**
open/closed **opið/lokað**
vacant/occupied **laus/upptekinn**
early/late **snemma/seint**

M

MAPS

Good maps are helpful to explore Iceland properly, and there are a large number available. Tourist offices have leaflets with basic maps and also sell more detailed ones. The best maps are those published by Ferðakort Ísland (www.ferdakort.is), based on data from the Icelandic National Land Survey, *Landmælingar Íslands*. These include a 1:200,000 road atlas of the whole country, a 1:500,000 touring map, a series of five 1:250,000 sheets covering all regions, and nine 'special maps' of the national parks and popular tourist areas at various scales.

MEDIA

There are English-language newspapers and magazines available on sale in Reykjavík one or two days after publication. They can also be found in public libraries (*bókasafn*).

The magazine *Iceland Review* (www.icelandreview.com) is published in English with informative articles and great photographs.

The *Reykjavík Grapevine* (http://grapevine.is) is an irreverent, free English-language newspaper containing articles, reviews and listings, and is available wherever there are tourists.

The government-owned RÚV and pay channels SkjárEinn and Stöð 2 are the most widely watched home grown TV channels in Iceland. Many hotels offer satellite TV giving direct access to international news and entertainment channels including CNN and the BBC.

MONEY (See also Budgeting for your Trip)

The Icelandic currency is the króna (ISK; plural: krónur), divided into 100 aurar. Notes are in denominations of ISK5,000, 2,000, 1,000 and 500, coins in denominations of ISK100, 50, 10, 5 and 1.

Currency Exchange. Banks will change foreign currency or travellers cheques – US dollars, sterling and euros are all easily exchanged. Outside normal banking hours you can exchange money at major hotels. There are 24-hour exchange facilities available at Keflavík Airport: look for **Landsbankinn** in the arrival hall for arriving passengers; on the second level for departing passengers.

At the time of going to press, the rate of exchange was as follows: £1 = ISK154; E1 = ISK132; $1 = ISK116.

Credit Cards. Credit cards are used everywhere in Iceland, with the most ubiquitous being Visa and MasterCard/EuroPay. American Express, JCB and Diners are far less common.

Cash advances are available on Visa and MasterCard/EuroPay from all banks, savings banks and automatic cash machines.

ATMs. The simplest way to obtain Icelandic krónur is from an ATM cash machine – plentiful in Reykjavík and other Icelandic towns. There are cash machines at the airport and at many banks. The charges will depend on your bank, but the rate of exchange is generally better than any other method.

Travellers Cheques. Hotels will exchange travellers cheques and banknotes for guests, at a rate slightly below the bank rate, depending on the availability of cash in the till.

O

OPENING TIMES

Shops, banks and other services rarely close for lunch. The following are rough guides to opening times in Reykjavík; opening times elsewhere in the country are usually shorter than this.

Banks: Mon–Fri 9.15am–4pm.

Post Offices: Mon–Fri 9am–6pm.

Shops: Mon–Fri 9am–6pm, Sat 10am–1pm/2pm/3pm/4pm. Smaller shops may not open until 10am. Some supermarkets open until 11pm daily.

Liquor Stores: Reykjavík: Mon–Thur 11am–6pm, Fri 11am–7pm, Sat 11am–6pm. Other stores usually much shorter hours – see www.vinbudin.is for details.

P

POLICE

In such a law-abiding country the police keep a low profile, and you are unlikely to come across them unless you commit a motoring offence. They can normally speak some English.

Police Emergency Number, tel: **112**.

Reykjavík Police Headquarters is at Hverfisgata 113–115, tel: 444 1000. The Reykjavík city-centre police station is at Tryggvagata 19, tel: 569 9025. For lost property, contact the police headquarters, tel: 444 1000 (open Mon–Fri 8.15am–4pm).

POST OFFICES

The Icelandic postal service is efficient, and there are post offices (Mon–Fri 9am–6pm) in every town. The Central Post Office

on Posthússtræti 5 (near the main square Austurvöllur) in Reykjavík is open Mon–Frid 9am–6pm, June, July and August Saturday 10am–2pm.

It takes up to six days for post to reach Europe or North America
and 10 days for Australia, New Zealand and South Africa.

Letters are sent by either priority (A) or economy (B) service, but
delivery time abroad is not noticeably different between the two
services. Airmail letters or postcards to Europe cost ISK180 (A) or
ISK165 (B); to other areas they are ISK240 (A) or ISK210 (B). There
are up-to-date prices and information at www.postur.is.

PUBLIC HOLIDAYS

The following are public holidays in Iceland. Note that most businesses, banks and shops will be closed on these days, and public
transport will be more limited than usual.

Fixed dates:
1 January New Year's Day
1 May Labour Day
17 June National Day
24 December Christmas Eve (from noon)
25 December Christmas Day
26 December Boxing Day
31 December New Year's Eve (from noon)
Movable dates:
Maundy Thursday
Good Friday
Easter Sunday
Easter Monday
First day of summer (first Thursday after 18 April)
Ascension Day
Whit Sunday
Whit Monday
Bank Holiday Monday (first Monday in August)

T

TELEPHONES

The code for Iceland is +354, followed by a seven-digit number. There are no area codes. To call abroad from Iceland, dial 00, plus the country code.

Payphones are becoming rare, but can still be found in post offices, petrol stations, swimming pools, shopping malls and transport hubs. These take coins or phone cards, which can be bought at kiosks or post offices in various denominations.

The four main GSM operators in Iceland are Siminn, Vodafone, TAL and Nova. Pre-paid SIM cards can be bought at filling stations. Useful numbers are as follows:

1811: international directory enquiries
118: national directory assistance

TIME ZONES

Iceland is on GMT all year round. Time in summer is as below.

Los Angeles	Chicago	New York	**Iceland**	London	Sydney
5am	7am	8am	**noon**	1pm	10pm

TIPPING

Service is always included in the bill, so tipping is not normally required. It is not usual to tip taxi drivers.

TOILETS

Public toilets are a rarity: there is one on Ingólfstorg (close to the tourist office); one at the top of Frakkastígur (close to Hallgrímskirkja); one on Vegamótastígur; and one at the end of Lækjargata (near the northeast corner of Tjörnin). It is better to make use of the facilities at your accommodation or at a bar or café.

TOURIST INFORMATION

The tourist information structure in Iceland is a little complex. The Icelandic Tourist Board (Geirsgata 9, Reykjavík 101, tel: 535 5500, www.ferdamalastofa.is/en) promotes Iceland abroad. The regional Tourist Information Centres are separately run, and some parts of the country also have Marketing Agencies. Staff speak excellent English and are usually very helpful. Opening times vary, but in summer they open early and close around 7pm.

The Tourist Information Centre in Reykjavík is at Aðalstræti 2, tel: 590 1550, www.visitreykjavik.is (daily 8am–8pm).

In Akureyri, the Tourist Information Centre is at Hof Menningarhús (Hof Culture House), Strandgata 12, weekdays 8am–4pm; tel: 450 1050, www.visitakureyri.is.

Information can be obtained worldwide from www.visiticeland.com.

TRANSPORT

Buses. There is an excellent system of buses both in Reykjavík (run by the Reykjavík bus company Strætó) and across the country. In the capital there are two terminals for the yellow city buses, one near the harbour at Lækjartorg, at the junction of Lækjargata and Austurstræti, the other at Hlemmur, at the far end of the main shopping street, Laugavegur. Maps showing all the routes are available from terminals, tourist offices, and at www.straeto.is.

Service times vary slightly from route to route, but generally buses run Mon–Fri 7am–midnight, Sat 8am–midnight and Sun 10am–midnight. There is a flat fare of ISK420, which must be paid in exact change as you board. If you are changing buses ask for a *skiftimiði*, which is valid on all buses for around 75 minutes. The Reykjavík City Card (see page 31) offers free unlimited travel for 24 (ISK3,500), 48 (ISK4,700) or 72 hours (ISK5,500).

Long-distance buses operate from the BSÍ Coach Terminal, Vatnsmýrarvegur (tel: 562 1011, www.bsi.is). There are a variety of 'bus passports' available if you are going to use the bus network extensively, and they come with different time limits.

Taxis. Taxis are available in all the major towns and cost about ISK1,600 for 3km (1.86 miles). There are ranks in Reykjavík on Lækjargata and Eiríksgata. To order a cab by phone call: Borgarbílastöðin (www.borgarbilastodin.is), tel: 552 2440; BSR (https://bsr.is/#/), tel: 561 0000; or Hreyfill-Bæjarleiðir (www.hreyfill.is) , tel: 588 5522.

Flights. Air Iceland (tel: 570 3030, www.airiceland.is) is the biggest domestic carrier, running flights from Reykjavík to Akureyri, Ísafjörður, and Egilsstaðir; and from Akureyri to Grímsey, Þórshöfn and Vopnafjörður. Eagle Air (Flugfélag Ernir, tel: 562 2640, www.eagleair.is) also operates internal flights from Reykjavík to Bíldudalur and Gjögur in the West Fjords, Húsavík, Höfn and the Westman Islands.

Ferries. The ferry Herjólfur runs to the Westman Islands (tel: 481 2800, www.herjolfur.is), from Landeyjahöfn near Hvollsvöllur on the south coast, or from Þorlákshöfn in bad weather – check sailings before travel. Sæferðir (Smiðjustígur 3, 340 Stykkisholmur, tel: 433 2254, www.seatours.is) runs the ferry Baldur, which sails to the West Fjords, as well as whale-watching tours and other excursions. *Sæfari* sails from Dalvík to Grímsey (via Hrisey) in the summer (Landflutningar-Samskip, Ranarbraut 2b, 620 Dalvík, tel: 458 8970, 853 2211, www.landflutningar.is/saefari).

Train Travel. There are no trains in Iceland.

V

VISAS AND ENTRY REQUIREMENTS

Iceland is a signatory to the Schengen Agreement, so, in principle, residents of other Schengen countries (Norway plus all EU countries except Britain and Ireland) can enter the country with national identity cards rather than passports. Flights from the UK go through passport control. Iceland doesn't require visas from citizens of EU states, the US, Canada, Australia or New Zealand; South African citizens do require one. The normal entry stamp in your passport is valid for a stay of up to three months, and your passport must be valid for a further three months beyond your proposed departure date. There are no currency restrictions.

WEBSITES AND INTERNET ACCESS

Websites. The websites for Iceland's regional tourist offices are:

www.east.is

www.northiceland.is

www.south.is

www.west.is

www.westfjords.is

www.visitreykjavik.is

Other useful sites include:

www.vedur.is Latest weather in Iceland

www.whatson.is Reykjavík events guide

www.bsi.is Icelandic bus times

Internet Access. Most cafés and bars in Reykjavík have Wi-fi, so if you are travelling with your own laptop, you can access the web for the price of a coffee.

YOUTH HOSTELS

Hostelling International (Borgartún 6, 105 Reykjavík, tel: 575 6700, e-mail: info@hostel.is, www.hostel.is) has 32 excellent hostels from which to choose. These are very popular and fill up quickly, so always book ahead. Most hostels have two- to six-bed rooms and family rooms. Duvets and pillows are complimentary. You can use your own sleeping-bag/linen or hire what you need from the hostel. A single bed in a dormitory will cost a member/non-member ISK4,050/4,750. The association also offers good deals on car hire and excursions.

RECOMMENDED HOTELS

The range of hotel and hostel accommodation in Iceland is very wide indeed. In Reykjavík there are some very stylish, world-class hotels – with prices to match. Elsewhere in the country, there are few hotels of genuine character, but what is lacking in terms of ambience is usually more than compensated by a stunning location. At the top end of the market, most hotels are fairly standard airport-style establishments. There is a reasonable selection of smaller, family-run hotels and guesthouses throughout the country, as well as budget accommodation for backpackers and hikers. Some schools double up as tourist accommodation during the holidays too, which can be a very cost-effective option.

High season is usually from the beginning of May until the beginning of September, when prices often double, and rooms can be hard to come by. From the end of September some places close altogether, although you should be able to find a room in most towns. The bigger hotels are increasingly offering special activities, such as snowmobiling, to attract visitors out of season.

Some organisations such as Hostelling International (www.hostel.is) and Icelandic Farm Holidays (www.farmholidays.is) publish annual brochures listing details of their accommodations. The free brochure *Áning*, available from tourist offices, lists around 200 hotels and guesthouses countrywide, as well as 50 campsites. Links can also be found on the website of the Icelandic Tourist Board (www.visiticeland.com).

The price guidelines below are for a double room with bathroom in high season, including breakfast and tax, unless otherwise stated. Hotels usually accept payment by credit card, but payment for guesthouses, farms, hostels and camp sites is generally by cash only. For making reservations, Iceland's country code is 354 (there are no local codes in Iceland).

$$$$	over ISK30,000
$$$	ISK23,000–30,000
$$	ISK15,000–22,000
$	below ISK15,000

Centerhotel Arnarhvoll $$$$ *Ingólfsstræti 1, tel: 595 8540,* www. centerhotels.is. Arnarhvoll is cool, clean, and has stunning views of the Harpa concert hall and across the bay. Five minutes' walk from the bar and restaurant action on Laugavegur. The same family runs four other Centerhotels, all in conveniently central locations.

Hótel Borg $$$$ *Pósthússtræti 11, tel: 551 1440,* www.hotelborg. is. This imposing building close to the Parliament was the city's first hotel. Beautifully renovated in modern style, with nods to its Art Deco heritage.

Hótel Cabin $$ *Borgartún 32, tel: 511 6030,* www.hotelcabin.is. Hótel Cabin is located a little out of the centre but upper-storey rooms have terrific views over the bay. Standard rooms are very small, but they are great value for Reykjavík.

Hótel Holt $$$$ *Bergstaðastræti 37, tel: 552 5700,* www.holt.is. This hotel is very elegant and comfortable, with great character and style. The public areas are an art-lover's delight, with the largest private collection of Icelandic paintings in existence. The rooms are well equipped, if a little small, and the restaurant is superb. It is also well known for having one of the finest ranges of whiskies in the country.

Icelandair Hotel Reykjavík Marina $$$$ *Mýrargata 2, tel: 444 4000, 560 8000,* www.icelandairhotels.com. The Icelandair Hotel hotel has been knocking the socks off its guests with its laidback ambience and quirky decor. It is worth splashing out for one of the larger deluxe rooms: those on the harbour side have interesting views over a working shipyard. At the time of writing, the Marina bar was the in-vogue place to see and be seen.

Hótel Leifur Eríksson $$$ *Skólavörðustígur 45, tel: 562 0800,* www.hotelleifur.is. The hotel has a prime location right opposite the Hallgrímskirkja church. This is a friendly family-run place with basic but comfortable rooms. There is no restaurant, although a continental breakfast is included and hot drinks are available 24 hours a day.

Luna Hotel Apartments $$$$ *Spítalastígur 1, Laufásvegur 6, Amt-mannsstígur 5, tel: 511 2800*, www.luna.is. These beautifully stylish apartments (for 1 to 4 people) are located over three buildings, dotted around a pleasant residential district a few blocks from Laugavegur. Check-in for all three is at Baldursgata 36.

Óðinsvé $$$$ *Óðinstorg 11, tel: 511 6200*, www.hotelodinsve.is. The pleasant, relaxed atmosphere makes this hotel, in a quiet residential quarter close to the centre, a comfortable place to stay. All rooms have tasteful Scandinavian decor, but deluxe rooms with split levels are the business.

Radisson Blu 1919 Hotel $$$$ *Pósthússtræti 2, tel: 599 1000*, www.radissonblu.com/1919hotel-reykjavik. Housed in the elegant former headquarters of the Eimskip shipping company, this hotel offers style and elegance right in the heart of the city and is one of the most sought-after addresses in which to stay. Old-fashioned charm meets Nordic chic.

Hótel Reykjavík Centrum $$$$ *Aðalstræti 16, tel: 514 6000*, www.hotelcentrum.is. Built above Reykjavík's oldest (Viking) house, there is nothing archaic about this airy modern hotel. Comfortable rooms with the city on the doorstep.

Reykjavík Loft Youth Hostel $$ *Bankastræti 7, tel: 553 8140*, www.lofthostel.is. Hostelling International Iceland opened a third Reykjavík hostel in 2013. This smart addition is central, with sunny staff, spacious rooms, free Wi-fi and a clean, green, ethical stance.

Room with a View $$$ *Laugavegur 18, tel: 552 7262*, www.roomwithaview.is. For a good, cost-effective alternative to a hotel, try these comfortable serviced apartments on the main shopping street. There is quite a lot of variety, from small basement studios to a 12-bed beast – check the website for further details.

Salvation Army Guesthouse $ *Kirkjustræti 2, tel: 561 3203*. The cheapest guesthouse in Reykjavík opens June to August only. It may be no-frills, but this hostel-style place is neat and clean and the central location is excellent. Single, double and triple rooms, and sleeping bag accommodation. There are facilities for cooking on the ground floor.

Three Sisters Guesthouse $$$ *Ránargata 16, tel: 565 2181,* www. threesisters.is. A splendid alternative to a hotel room, these cosy studio apartments near the harbour come with bedrooms and kitchenettes.

SOUTH AND SOUTHEAST

Hótel Eldhestar $$$$ *Vellir, 810 Hveragerði, tel: 480 4800,* http://eld hestar.is. As well as offering riding tours, Eldhestar horse farm has a lovely one-storey wooden eco-hotel attached. Rooms are comfortable, with direct access to the garden, and there are log fires in the communal areas. There is full disabled access.

Hótel Geysir $$$ *Haukadalur, 801 Selfoss, tel: 480 6800,* www. geysircenter.is. Located right next to the world-famous geysers, this is a friendly, family-run establishment and gets very busy with tour groups in high season. There are hot tubs (accessible in summer only) and an outdoor pool. Horse-riding and quad-bike tours offered.

Hali Country Hotel $$$$ *Hali, 781 Hornafjörður, tel: 478 1073,* http:// hali.is. Once the farm of writer Þórbergur Þórðarson, this lovely seaside spot near to Jökulsárlón glacial lagoon offers guests 18 clean, quiet rooms and an excellent restaurant, serving char from the pool over the road. It is easy to spot – just look out for the row of giant books!

Hótel Hvolsvöllur $$$ *Hlíðarvegur 7, 860 Hvolsvöllur, tel: 487 8050,* www.hotelhvolsvollur.is. This hotel near the Saga Centre may have seen better days, but staff are friendly and it is very handy for the ferry service to the Westman Islands.

Icelandair Hotel Klaustur $$$ *Klausturvegur 6, Kirkjubæjarklaustur, tel: 487 4900,* www.icelandairhotels.com. Part of the Icelandair chain, Hotel Klaustur makes up for some unusually basic rooms with an excellent restaurant. In a town with literally one street, Klaustur still makes a good stay: there is nothing else to this standard for some distance around. Out of season you could find you have the whole place to yourself.

Hótel Ion $$$$ *off Rd 360, Nesjavellir, tel: 482 3415*, www.ioniceland.is. This hotel has an otherworldly setting, in the middle of steaming lava fields overlooking Nesjavellir geothermal plant – private transport is vital. It makes a good base for exploring the Golden Circle. Extras include an outdoor hot tub, sauna and spa treatments.

Puffin Hótel $$$ *Víkurbraut 26, Vík, tel: 487 1212*. A delightful little place with a cosy dining room and bar. Lundi means puffin in Icelandic, and the owners, who are great nature enthusiasts, will be more than happy to tell you where to go and see the real things. The hotel also offers cheaper hostel-style accommodation (**$**) next door.

Hótel Vestmannaeyjar $$$ *Vestmannabraut 28, Heimaey, Westman Islands, tel: 481 2900*, www.hotelvestmannaeyjar.is. A comfortable small-town hotel, where you're made to feel like an old friend as soon as you step through the door. The hotel is also the reception for the HI hostel Sunnuhóll (**$**), round the back.

EAST AND NORTHEAST

Gistihúsið Egilsstöðum $$$ *Egilsstaðir, tel: 471 1114*, www.egilsstadir.com. This converted stone farmhouse aims to recreate the atmosphere of early 20th-century rural Iceland. The building dates from 1903, and its parlour and collection of period artefacts all add to the effect. It's just west of the town on the shores of Lake Lagarfljót. There are horses in the paddock.

Guesthouse Gula Villan $$ *Brekkugata 8, Akureyri, tel: 896 8464*, www.gulavillan.is. Pleasant, sunny, family-run guesthouse in the town centre, with a second house acting as an overflow at busy times. Some of the spacious rooms have private bathrooms, the rest have neat, clean, shared facilities. Also has sleeping-bag accommodation (**$**) and kitchens available for guest use.

Hótel Hérað $$$$ *Miðvangur 1–7, Egilsstaðir, tel: 444 4000,* www. icelandairhotels.com. Part of the Icelandair chain, this smart, renovated hotel is a welcome sight after a long day hiking.

Kaldbaks Kot $$ *Kaldbakur, Húsavík, tel: 892 1744,* www.cottages.is. These snug log cabins, overlooking the sea one mile from Húsavík, make the perfect base for self-caterers: they have large terraces, and contain all the facilities you need, plus there are ample hot pots from which you can enjoy the idyllic surroundings.

Hótel Kea $$$$ *Hafnarstræti 87–9, Akureyri, tel: 460 2000,* www.hotel kea.is. A reliable and comfortable hotel in Akureyri, close to all the town's restaurants and shops. The rooms have mini-bars and satellite television, and there is free internet access in the lobby. The company also owns the cheaper Hótel Norðurland (tel: 462 2600), next door.

Hótel Reynihlíð $$$$ *Reynihlíð, 660 Reykjahlíð, tel: 464 4170,* www. reynihlid.is. Lake Mývatn attracts hordes of tourists, and accommodation is limited and expensive. This long-standing hotel is one of the best options: newer rooms are smart and modern, and there is a lovely, lively café-bar in the adjoining Old Farm building. It is important to book well ahead in high season. The hotel also offers accommodation in the sweet little nine-roomed Hótel Reykjahlíð, perfectly situated on the lakeside.

WEST AND NORTHWEST

Borgarnes B&B $$ *Skúlagötu 21, 310 Borgarnes, tel: 434 1566, 842 5866,* www.borgarnesbb.is. Set in a beautiful old house by the sea in Borgarnes, overlooking Englendingavík (Englishman's Bay). There's a fine, friendly welcome, a breakfast boasting pancakes and home-baked bread, and a guest kitchen for self-caterers. Note that all rooms are twins.

Hótel Djúpavík $ *Djúpavík, 524 Árneshreppur, tel: 451 4037,* www. djupavik.com. In the remote village of Djúpavík, this memorable spot was once the women's accommodation for a former herring-processing plant. It now makes for a typically quirky Icelandic farm-stay, with small rooms and shared bathrooms, a warm welcome, home-cooked food and a fascinating historic milieu.

Gamla Gistihúsið $$** *Mánagata 5, 400 Ísafjörður, tel: 456 4146,* http://isafjordurhotels.is/gamla/. A sweet-and-sunny guesthouse in the middle of the Old Town, with shared bathrooms, but with washbasins in the rooms. Also has sleeping bag accommodation (**$) in a second house on the same street, with cooking facilities.

Fosshótel Reykholt $$$ *Reykholt, tel: 435 1260,* www.fosshotel.is. Surrounded by rolling countryside and enjoying one of the most historic locations in western Iceland, Reykholt's only accommodation option is perfectly placed for visiting the former home of saga writer Snorri Sturluson.

Hótel Ísafjörður $$$ *Silfurtorg 2, 400 Ísafjörður, tel: 456 4111,* www.hotelisafjordur.is. Right in the town centre. Standard rooms are average; it's worth paying extra for deluxe. The highlight is the good restaurant with its fine fjord views. The owners also run the summer-only Edda Hotel.

Hótel Reykjanes $–$$ *tel: 456 4844,* http://reykjaneswestfjords.is. Spectacular views across the fjord from a utilitarian hotel, with shared bathrooms; sleeping-bag accommodation and camping are also available. The high point is the 50-metre (165ft) swimming pool, fed by hot spring waters.

Hótel Arctic Tindastóll $$$ *Lindargata 3, Sauðárkrókur, tel: 453 5002,* www.arctichotels.is. Built in 1884, Hótel Tindastóll is not only the oldest hotel in Iceland but also one of the most unusual. Its stone walls and timber beams retain a great sense of history, and antique artefacts are dotted throughout. Every room is a good size with modern amenities. Marlene Dietrich stayed here while entertaining the troops during World War II.

INDEX

Þingeyrar 71
Þingvellir 41
Þórisvatn lake 87
Þórshöfn 73
Þórsmörk 57

Akranes 46
Akureyri 63
    Akureyrarkirkja 65
    Akureyri Municipal
        Museum 66
    Art Museum 66
    Botanical Gardens
        65
    Hafnarstræti 64
    Nonnahús 66
Ásbyrgi canyon 80

Blue Lagoon
    (Bláa Lónið) 39
Bolungarvík 50
Borgarnes 46
Breiðamerkurjökull
    62

Dalvík 67
Dettifoss 80
Dimmuborgir basin 77
Djúpivogur 84
Dynjandi waterfall 52

Egilsstaðir 81
Eiríksstaðir farm 48
Eskifjörður 84
Eyjafjörður 67

Flatey island (west
    coast) 49

Geysir 44
Goðafoss 74
Grímsey island 67
    Sandvík 68
Grótagjá 76
Gullfoss 44

Hafnarfjörður 38
Hallormsstaður 82
Heimaey 54
Hnjótur 53
Höfn 62
Hófsós 69
Hólar í Hjaltadal 70
Hólmanes nature reserve
    84
Hornstrandir Peninsula 51
Hrafnseyri 52
Hraunfossar 47
Húsafell 47
Húsavík 71
Hvannadalshnúkur 61
Hveravellir 89

Ísafjörður 50

Jarðböðin 78
Jökulsárlón 62

Kaldalón glacial lagoon 51
Kirkjubæjarklaustur 59
Kjarnaskógur forest 67
Kjölur Route 88
Krafla volcano 78
Kristínartindur 61

Lakagígar Crater Row 60
Lake Mývatn 74
Landmannalaugar 88
Largarfljót River 82
Látrabjarg 52
Laufás 69
Laxá River 74
Leirbotn power station 78
Lögurinn lake 82
Lundey island (west
    coast) 38

Mt Hekla 56
Mt Helgafell 49
Mt Snæfell (Eastern
    Iceland) 82

Neskaupstaður 83

Ólafsvík 48

Papey island 84

Rauðasandur 53
Reyðarfjörður 84
Reykholt 46
Reykjahlið 75
Reykjanes 51
Reykjavík 4, 11
    Alþingishúsið 30
    Árbæjarsafn 38
    Ásmundarsafn 34
    Austurvöllur 30
    Culture House 29
    Dómkirkjan 30
    Fálkahúsið 33
    Government House
        29
    Hafnarhús 33
    Hallgrímskirkja 26
    Höfði House 35
    Kjarvalsstaðir 36
    Lækjartorg 30
    Laugardalur 36
    Laugavegur 28
    Listasafn Íslands 31
    Nauthólsvík beach
        35
    Norræna Húsið 34
    Öskjuhlíð hill 34
    Perlan (Pearl) 34
    Raðhús (City Hall)
        31
    Safn Einars Jónssonar
        28
    Sögusafnið 34
    Tjörnin lake 31
    Þjóðmenningarhúsið
        29
    Þjóðminjasafn Íslands
        34
Reynisdrangar 59

Sandvík 68
Selfoss 80
Seyðisfjörður 83
Sjálfskapar Viti crater 79
Skálholt 43
Skógar 58
Skútustaðir 77
Smjörfjöll 73
Snæfellsjökull glacier 48

Snorralaug 47
Sprengisandur Route 86
Storagjá 76
Stóri-Laugardalur 52
Strokkur 44
Stykkishólmur 48
Svalbarðseyri 69
Svartifoss 62

Tálknafjörður 52

Vatnajökull glacier 60
Viðey 37
Vík 59
Vindbelgjarfjall 77
Viti crater 78

Westman Islands 53

INSIGHT ⊙ GUIDES POCKET GUIDE

ICELAND

First Edition 2017

Editor: Tom Fleming
Author: Lance Price and James Proctor
Head of Production: Rebeka Davies
Picture Editor: Tom Smyth
Cartography Update: Carte
Update Production: AM Services
Photography Credits: Alamy 6MC, 19, 88;
Dreamstime 44, 61, 64, 69, 86, 87, 89; Fotolia
48, 73; Getty Images 4ML, 4TL, 5M, 7T, 11, 17,
24, 36, 55, 94, 96, 102; iStock 4MC, 5M, 47, 57,
58, 59, 97; Ming Tang-Evans/Apa Publications
4TC, 5TC, 6TL, 6TL, 7M, 7MC, 7T, 8L, 8R, 9,
9R, 13, 15, 21, 26, 27, 28, 29, 30, 32, 33, 35,
38, 41, 43, 45, 49, 50, 51, 52, 53, 54, 60, 63, 65,
66, 70, 74, 75, 77, 79, 81, 83, 84, 85, 90, 99,
101, 105, 106; Shutterstock 5T, 5MC, 6ML, 93;
SuperStock 7M
Cover Picture: Shutterstock

**Special Sales, Content Licensing
and CoPublishing**
Insight Guides can be purchased in bulk
quantities at discounted prices. We can create
special editions, personalised jackets and
corporate imprints tailored to your needs.
sales@insightguides.com;
www.insightguides.biz

All Rights Reserved
© 2017 Apa Digital (CH) AG and
Apa Publications (UK) Ltd

Printed in China by CTPS

Contact us
Every effort has been made to provide
accurate information in this publication,
but changes are inevitable. The publisher
cannot be responsible for any resulting loss,
inconvenience or injury. We would appreciate
it if readers would call our attention to any
errors or outdated information. We also
welcome your suggestions; please contact us
at: hello@insightguides.com
www.insightguides.com

Distribution
UK, Ireland and Europe: Apa Publications
(UK) Ltd; sales@insightguides.com
United States and Canada: Ingram Publisher
Services; ips@ingramcontent.com
Australia and New Zealand: Woodslane;
info@woodslane.com.au
Southeast Asia: Apa Publications (SN) Pte;
singaporeoffice@insightguides.com
Worldwide: Apa Publications (UK) Ltd;
sales@insightguides.com

Berlitz®

speaking your language

phrase book & dictionary
phrase book & CD

Available in: Arabic, Brazilian Portuguese*, Burmese*, Cantonese
Chinese, Croatian, Czech*, Danish*, Dutch, English, Filipino, Finnish*, French,
German, Greek, Hebrew*, Hindi*, Hungarian*, Indonesian, Italian, Japanese,
Korean, Latin American Spanish, Malay, Mandarin Chinese, Mexican Spanish,
Norwegian, Polish, Portuguese, Romanian*, Russian, Spanish, Swedish, Thai,
Turkish, Vietnamese
*Book only